*Twayne's English Authors Series*

EDITOR OF THIS VOLUME

Sylvia E. Bowman
*Indiana University*

# Thomas Carlyle

**TEAS 238**

# THOMAS CARLYLE

By WALTER WARING
*Kalamazoo College*

**TWAYNE PUBLISHERS**
A DIVISION OF G. K. HALL & CO., BOSTON

**Library of Congress Cataloging in Publication Data**

Waring, Walter, 1917 -
Thomas Carlyle.

(Twayne's English authors series ; TEAS 238)
Bibliography: p. 139-43.
Includes index.
1. Carlyle, Thomas, 1795 - 1881—Criticism and interpretation.
PR4434.W37        824'.8        78-840
ISBN 0-8057-6710-X

Frontispiece photo of Thomas Carlyle taken
about 1860 by Elliot and Fry

# *Contents*

## About the Author

Walter Waring, director of humanities at Kalamazoo College, Kalamazoo, Michigan, was formerly professor of English and chairman of the department at that institution.

A scholar-teacher of wide interests, Waring is a lecturer, a painter of oils and watercolors, and the author of many reviews.

# *Preface*

Among writers of the nineteenth century, Carlyle was singular in that both friends and enemies viewed him inaccurately. Regarded as a saint by some and as a satanist by others, his real message is largely ignored. During the years of World War II, many readers mistakenly took him as a fascist. More recently the tendency has been to see him as a literary figure. None of these views is accurate. Although he counted among his friends many literary people, Carlyle was largely indifferent to most of what the term suggests. His view of history, economics, and the social milieu is that of the moralist. He escapes the praise of those who see him as a traditionalist by his forthright attacks on traditions, which he views as worn out social garments; and he escapes the censure of those who regard him as a spokesman of "might makes right" by giving might only to the hero who is certified by the process of *entsagen*.

The purpose of this volume is to show how Carlyle was shaped by his environment, by the faith that dominated his family, and by his discovery of a method with which he could contend with his times without essentially modifying the commitments inculcated in him during his childhood. The first two chapters include a brief review of the larger setting of his youth and of his childhood and education. The remaining sections treat his writing as the discovery and expression of the principles that seem to guide his work throughout his life.

W. W. WARING

*Kalamazoo College*

# Chronology

1795  Thomas Carlyle born at Ecclefechan, December 4.

1809  Goes to Edinburgh University in November; plans to enter ministry.

1814  Becomes tutor of mathematics at Annan School.

1815  Becomes schoolmaster at Kirkcaldy in autumn term.

1818  Leaves teaching; returns to Edinburgh in November. Tutors privately.

1819  Studies German. Considers law as possible profession.

1820  Studies German. Writes first published essays for *Edinburgh Encyclopedia*.

1821  Meets Jane Welsh in May.

1823  Publishes *Schiller* in *London Magazine*.

1824  Visits Coleridge at Highgate. Visits Paris in autumn.

1826  Marries Jane Welsh. Settles at Comely Bank, Edinburgh.

1827  Publishes first article in *Edinburgh Review* and *German Romance*.

1828  Moves to Craigenputtock. Meets J. S. Mill.

1832  Father dies. Göethe dies.

1833  *Sartor Resartus* to appear in *Frazer's Magazine*.

1834  Begins *French Revolution*.

1835  Manuscripts of *French Revolution* burned at J. S. Mill's home.

1837  Completes rewriting of *French Revolution* in January. Lectures on German literature in the spring.

1838  *Sartor Resartus, Miscellanies* published in book form.

1840  Aids in foundation of London Library. Reading for *Cromwell*.

1841  Publishes *Heroes and Hero-Worship*.

1842  Visits continent. Writing *Past and Present*.

1843  Publishes *Past and Present*.

1845  Publishes *Cromwell*.

1845  Corn Law abolished.

1850  *Latter-Day Pamphlets* published.

1851  Writes *Life of Sterling*.

1854  Begins *Frederick*.

1857     Finishes first two Volumes of *Frederick*. Tours Germany.

1862     Publishes Volume III of *Frederick*.

1864     Publishes Volume IV of *Frederick*.

1865     Completes *Frederick*. Volumes V and VI published. Appointed Rector of Edinburgh University.

1866     Jane Carlyle dies.

1872     Writing *Early Kings of Norway*.

1874     Receives Prussian Order of Merit.

1875     Declines a baronetcy.

1881     Dies February 5.

# CHAPTER 1

# The Background

## I  The Setting

WHEN Thomas Carlyle was born in 1795, England was in the midst of social and economic revolutions that were making her the first modern industrial nation. Hargreaves' spinning jenny (1769), Crompton's mule (1779), and Kay's flying shuttle (1783) had revolutionized the weaving of cloth. The applications of steam to work the looms and spinning devices was the first step in a process destined to change every aspect of human existence. By 1795, Manchester had become a center for the manufacture of cloth by the new machines, and changes in occupation faced many families who until this time had earned a few shillings a week spinning and weaving by hand as a part of their regular household tasks. Hardest hit by machine production were the small farmers and villagers who grew most of what they ate and turned to spinning and weaving during the winter season as a means of supplementing their income. As the manufacture of cloth concentrated in the rapidly growing industrial centers, villagers and farmers, no longer able to compete with the efficiency of modern production, moved to the cities to swell the labor market.

The changes that occur in morality, politics, and economics when large numbers of a population move from the land to cities require little commentary for contemporary readers, who can see much the same process in their own century. At the end of the eighteenth century, however, England faced industrialization for the first time; and no man was able to anticipate its results. Predictions, optimistic or ominous, fell far short of actual changes. As the population moved from the countryside to the cities, pews were emptied in the country churches; but none were waiting to be filled near their new dwellings. The Church of England was unprepared for the type of reorganization required by the time. A man who left the parish of

11

his birth, where he nominally remained a member of the congregation, often left the church. Although the plight of the new laboring class—for that was what they were destined to become—was widely recognized, neither the local nor the national government was any better able to deal with the problem of mass movement than was the church. No precedent pointed the way to the solution of public welfare in the new society. Seemingly abandoned by church and state, the laboring class had no place in the existing social structure. Regarded as outsiders by the established city dweller, separated from friends and relatives, lonely and confused, they often lived in a misery of spirit exceeded only by their real physical degradation.

Wordsworth's "Michael," a poem describing the heartbreak of the parents of a boy who went to the city to make his fortune and pay off the family debt, tells a story that must have occurred many times over. At first the boy fulfilled his promise, but "at length, / He in the dissolute city gave himself / To evil courses; ignominy and shame / Fell on him, so that he was driven at last / To seek a hiding place beyond the seas."[1] For most, however, there was no escape from the miseries of industrialization. Men and women drawn to the factory towns by the promise of steady employment or by the hope of wealth found the work debilitating, the wages meager, and the condition of life unhealthy. Thousands of basement dwellings were built for Irish laborers who fled from famine in Ireland. One and two room quarters, often without windows until the repeal of the window tax in 1851, were common. Dwellings contained no provisions for water or for the disposal of waste. Frequently, twenty or more families were provided with a single outhouse and with a single source of water. No provisions were made for parks, playgrounds, schools, or churches. Often illiterate and usually without religious or political representation, the factory worker had no means by which to voice his misery or to communicate his needs.

Often the mother of a family spent twelve hours at piece work such as hemming or picking fur from rabbit pelts for the production of felt hats. She had little time or energy to care for her family. Even the products of more efficient production were beyond her means. The corn law of 1689 kept the price of bread high by offering the grower a bounty for every bushel of grain exported when the price in the English market was less than six shillings. In 1815, a protective tariff was placed upon imported grain to protect the price of English grain from foreign import; and during the years of 1816 and 1817, when crops were poor, the misery of the poor increased. Medical attention was hard to get and often ineffective when it was available. In desperation, the working mother sometimes administered an opium tonic to the hungry or ailing child, which served to quiet him during her hours at work or away from home.

Not all employers were indifferent to the fate of the working class. Robert Owen, an enlightened mill owner at New Lanark, reduced the working hours of adult workers from seventeen to ten, refused to employ children under nine, and provided schools for the children of laborers at company expense; but in general, William Godwin's doctrine that the interests of society were more important than the greed of the individual went unheeded. Legislation to protect the worker was slow in coming; and, when it was enacted, it was frequently without means of enforcement. Even had the means of enforcement been present, the industrial laborer's lot might not have improved greatly. His numbers were increasing so rapidly that by 1831 the population of England was half industrial and half agricultural. The rapid growth of the working class contributed greatly to its impoverishment.

On the other hand, life for the agricultural laborer was only a little less vile than for his city cousin. Although landed farmers were almost as prosperous as the new industrialists, the agricultural worker's chief advantage over the industrial worker was fresher air and purer food. Crop rotation, the enrichment of soil, and improved breeding practices were increasing production, but the small farmer who could not afford experimentation or who distrusted new methods did not share greatly in the increasing wealth of the country. W. E. Lunt in his *History of England* tells us that over three hundred thousand acres of land were fenced from 1700 to 1760, well over three million acres between 1761 and 1801, and by the middle of the nineteenth century nearly as many more.[2] Mandatory fencing of private property was disastrous to the cottagers and small farmers who could not prove ownership to the land they had used for generations. Often even when they had proof of ownership, they lost their lands because they were unable to pay for their share of the enclosure. Furthermore, when land was fenced, it was frequently redistributed. Owners of small farms often found themselves relocated on poorer or even smaller plots. As a result, many small farmers left the countryside, only to be added to the poor rolls or to swell the industrial labor market. Oliver Goldsmith's description of the plight of the poor agriculturist is not poetic exaggeration:

> Where then, ah where, shall Poverty reside,
> To 'scape the pressure of contiguous Pride,
> If to some common's fenceless limits strayed,
> He drives his flocks to pick the scanty blade,
> Those fenceless fields the sons of wealth divide,
> And even the bare-worn common is denied.[3]

The disappearance of common land left the small farmer as dispossessed and isolated as was the industrial worker. He, too, was without official spokesmen to voice his misery; and he often turned to poaching or hayburning in the same despair that drove his city cousin to gin or opium.

Between 1750 and 1850, Englishmen became increasingly aware of man's growing separation from the expectations that he had counted on for generations. Some of the heightened love and admiration for unspoiled nature during the early decades of the nineteenth century may be attributed to industrial activity and the growth of industrial populations. Painfully conscious of human degradation in his emerging society, the Englishman of the nineteenth century idealized the passing society, finding in it virtues of beauty, brotherhood, and godliness. Writers of the early decades of the nineteenth century looked to nature as the key to human salvation. Wordsworth discovered it to be a moral guide. Byron found it a responsive voice to human passion, and Keats on occasion used it as an escape for "one who has been long in city pent."[4] Carlyle regarded nature as the book of holy and immutable truth, readable only to the hero. Beyond these individual idealizations of nature lies the far more serious recognition of alienation from the new society into which they were thrust.

## II  *The Slogans*

Thus, industrialization resulted first of all in a cry for brotherly love. Although man could not return to a simple, pastoral life, he could affirm his brotherhood with his fellow sufferers. The revolutions in America and France and the turmoil in England were just as much efforts to escape utter loneliness and isolation as they were efforts to establish a sense of community and fellowship; but the slogan was brotherhood. Human relationships, traditionally vertical, became horizontal. Once man became a worker in a factory that produced cloth or pins, his master was the machine that he tended. His relationship to his employer was limited to the function

for which he was paid. Off duty, the worker's associates were men
in like situation, free to roam the streets or to tumble into a cot from
sheer exhaustion. No man sought his company or his opinion, his
love or his loyalty. He was paid in cash for the service he performed.
Where he lived, how he lived, and what he thought were his own
concerns as long as his service remained satisfactory.

Indifference to the fate of the common man had never been so
serious in England as in Europe. The nobility assumed special
rights, but it also undertook paternalistic responsibilities for those
who served. Furthermore, English letters had, on occasion,
represented the cause of human brotherhood since the time of
Chaucer, who in the fourteenth century brought a wide range of
classes into fellowship in his *Canterbury Tales*. Two hundred years
later, in his *Merchant of Venice*, William Shakespeare permitted
Shylock to enter a plea for the unpopular Jew:

He hath disgraced me, and hindered me half a million, laughed at my
losses, mocked at my gains, scorned my nation, thwarted my bargains, cool-
ed my friends, heated mine enemies. And what's his reason? I am a Jew.
Hath not a Jew eyes? Hath not a Jew hands, organs, dimensions, senses,
affections, passions? Fed with the same good, hurt with the same weapons,
subject to the same diseases, healed by the same means, warmed and cool-
ed by the same winter and summer as a Christian is?[5]

It is true that Shakespeare reserved the expression of such sen-
timents for characters who did not, in the last analysis, prevail.
Even so, as statements of man's brotherhood presented in the popular theater, they undoubtedly reached a broader audience than did
similar expressions of his nondramatic contemporaries. Montaigne
wrote a clear expression of human brotherhood in his "Apologie of
Raymond Sebond:" "The soules of Emperours and Coblers are all
cast in the same mould. Considering the importance of Princes' actions, and their weight, wee persuade ourselves, they are brought
forth by some as weighty and important causes; wee are deceived:
They are moved, stirred and removed in their motions, by the same
springs and wards, that wee are in ours."[6] Such ideas did not,
however, become urgent pronouncements until the end of the
eighteenth century.

As economic developments changed the patterns of life for mul-
titudes of men, women, and children, the ineffectiveness of the
traditional social structure became more apparent; and the calls for
human brotherhood carried overtones of revolt. In "Is There for

Honest Poverty," Robert Burns wrote, "It's comin yet for a' that, / That man to man, the world o'er, / Shall brithers be for a' that!"[7] A significant difference exists, however, between Burns' call for brotherhood in the late eighteenth century and its expression in the fellowship of Chaucer's pilgrims or in Shakespeare's Shylock. Chaucer's brotherhood crosses class in the common religious interest of the pilgrims. Shylock is requesting recognition as a human. Burns' brotherhood implies social and political reform.

Needless to say, the American and the French revolutions added the social and political dimensions to brotherhood in the slogans of the times, and liberty and equality soon became more important than brotherhood. Brotherhood, the one slogan that could conceivably exist in a society of classes, became less important as time passed. Writers of the early nineteenth century were more likely to emphasize liberty, as did Bryon, or equality, as did Shelley.

Nature, the fourth slogan of the period, underlies the first three because in a sense liberty, equality, and fraternity can be derived from special views of nature. If we regard nature as did Wordsworth in *The Prelude*, she becomes a moral teacher who knows men as brothers and who instructs them in brotherly harmony. If we look at nature as did Byron in *Childe Harold* or in *Manfred*, she reflects and encourages man's need for individual freedom to act. If we see her as Shelley saw her in *Prometheus Unbound*, "Ode to the West Wind," or "Ozymandias," she becomes a powerful agent for equality. If we view nature as did Keats in *Endymion* and in his great odes, she becomes the stimulator of the human senses and thus responsible for man's new thirst for sensational experience, the last of the great slogans of the nineteenth century.

In his search for an understanding of human knowledge, John Locke, the great seventeenth century rationalist, said, "Let us put the ideas of our mind, just as we put the things of the laboratory, to the test of experience."[8] Discovering that simple ideas, such as ideas of heat and cold, come from sensational experience, Locke searched for the source of ideas of beauty, justice, and love in experience. He concluded that these ideas are also derived from the human senses. Such conclusions were highly controversial during his life, but they became practical rules during the nineteenth century.

The acceptance of Locke's position was strengthened by the work of Jeremy Bentham and his younger associate James Mill. The vigor of these men established Bentham's pleasure-pain philosophy as a powerful view of reality. Although neither Mill nor Bentham had particular sympathy for the arts, literature responded readily to the pleasure-pain formula taught by their philosophy. Beginning in the eighteenth century with Mark Aikenside's *Pleasures of the Imagination* (1744) and reaching its height of popularity in Samuel Roger's *Pleasures of Memory* (1792) and in Campbell's *Pleasures of Hope* (1799), human sensation became a well-established basis for human values. Much of the prose and poetry written during the early years of the nineteenth century builds its values upon the evidence of human sensations.

Sensation as a basis for reality is not limited to literature. Its force is felt in all areas of human endeavor. In education, prizes were given to careful students and birchings were given to the indifferent. Medicine flourished because it could relieve men of pain, and mechanization increased because it relieved men of drudgery. Trade expanded to provide him with a greater variety of pleasures. Before long, men in all fields had found reasons to support the new way of thinking. As Bentham demonstrated that in the kingdom of senses all men are kings, Adam Smith's *Wealth of Nations* pointed the way to a larger distribution of the pleasures of ltfe by plotting an economic course for the new individualist.

## III  *Carlyle's Response to His Age*

The Enlightenment freed man from the fear of God and from the fear of his superiors, but it also introduced him to a loneliness sometimes more galling than the restraints that had been lost. For many, the result was unbearable personal suffering. Wordsworth suffered profound depression following his return to England from France in 1792. John Stuart Mill struggled with a similar experience from 1826 to 1829. Robert Burns, Charles Lamb, and Tom Moore used alcohol to escape. S. T. Coleridge and Thomas De Quincey turned to drugs. The lives of Byron and Shelley are marked by excesses. In fact, the more the writer responded to the issues of the day, the more his life is marked with evidence of personal disquietude. Thomas Carlyle endured mysterious stomach disorders throughout his life.

Even when the life of the writer appeared outwardly calm, his writing echoed the changing times. The restrained rhetoric of the eighteenth century was abandoned in favor of freer practices. Diction became sensational, connotative, and associational, expressing the increased importance of personal experience. Sentences were modified to conform more nearly to the patterns of speech. Tone and point of view became personal and direct. Literature turned from form to feeling. Kierkegaard in Denmark, Göethe in Germany, Byron in England, Carlyle in Scotland abandoned the rhetorical constraints of the past for a new expressiveness.

No eyes were quicker to observe changes and no ears were keener to hear new tones than those of Thomas Carlyle. During the course of his life, he resonded to all the issues of his time. What sets Carlyle apart from his contemporaries is the way in which he responded to the developments that were taking place around him. He so deplored the social changes that appeared with the machine age that even the word *machine* held evil connotations for him. He regarded the poverty, the idleness, and the crowding of growing industrial centers as a judgment of the Divine upon a people who had erred. He lamented the disappearance of the old skills and handicrafts that the machine age rendered obsolete, for he saw their passing as the final debasement of the sturdy craftsman who became a servant to the machine that had taken over his work. He despised the rising importance of cash payments for human service. He understood the calls for freedom as lawless disregard of authority and merit.

Carlyle was not primarily a social or political observer, even though what he saw and responded to most vividly were social and political developments. His analysis of the human situation lies almost entirely within a moral frame that seems curiously remote when compared to the humanism of Shakespeare or Montaigne. His view of the world bears the influence of his early training, the concerns of the time, and the temper of his mind. His life was deeply rooted in the pious home in which he was reared, in his youthful determination to enter the ministry, and ultimately in his vision of a universe ruled by God through His elected viceroys. Because they influenced greatly the direction Carlyle took and because they conditioned his responses to his own experiences, the condition and nature of his home and childhood require consideration.

### CHAPTER 2

# The Early Years

## I  *Home and Parents*

THOMAS Carlyle was born on December 4, 1795, to James and Margaret Aitkin Carlyle in the village of Ecclefechan, Annandale, Scotland. His father was by occupation a stonemason, who, after 1815, abandoned his trade to earn his livelihood as a small farmer. Margaret Aitkin, his mother, was James' second wife, his first, Janet, having died of a fever in 1792. Although James had little education, he could read and write and was known in the village as a good arithmetician. Margaret had even less education than her husband, though Thomas asserts that he learned to read by her instruction.

Writing in 1832, Thomas gives us what is perhaps the best clue to an understanding of his boyhood and ultimately the convictions of the man, in a description of his father James Carlyle.

"living and life-giving," he was, nevertheless, but half-developed. We all had to complain that we durst not freely love him. His heart seemed as if walled in; he had not the free means to unbosom himself. My mother has owned to me that she could never understand him; that her affection and (with all their little strifes) her admiration of him was obstructed. It seemed as if an atmosphere of fear repelled us from him. To me it was especially so. Till late years, when he began to respect me more, and, as it were, to look up to me for instruction, for protection (a relation unspeakably beautiful), I was ever more or less awed and chilled before him. My heart and tongue played freely only with my mother.[1]

Carlyle's uneasiness in his father's company may have been a result of James' moral and religious orientation. He was a devout Calvinist, convinced of man's sinful nature and of the corresponding wrath of God, who had ordained human life as a test of man's spiritual capabilities. Suspicious of pleasure, his life is a study of abnegation and sacrifice. For James Carlyle and his family, the Divine Will entered into human life daily, testing man's faith and fortitude in every situation. The troubles of daily life were seen as trials of Christian patience or as evidence of God's will, as were personal health or illness, poverty or prosperity. Life to James Carlyle was a moral drama that ended its final scene in heaven or in hell.

James' convictions permitted little time for gaiety and no time for frivolity. In the simple life of rural Scotland, the results of strict piety were heightened immeasurably. The social life of Ecclefechan, the birthplace and early home of Thomas Carlyle, was limited to the saloons of the village or to the church and the activities of the family, but the choice was even more restricted for James Carlyle's family. When a young man, James had joined the Burgher sect, linking his life permanently with a dissenting group who were known for narrow piety and dissatisfaction with the worldly ways of their friends and neighbors. Because of his stern, irascible nature, the family of James Carlyle rarely participated in social activities, though they were firmly bound together in work and worship. The history of the James Carlyle family is a story of their struggle to win a livelihood from a harsh land and peace from a jealous God. Carlyle himself summarizes his childhood when he writes in his *Reminiscences*, "We were all particularly taught that work (temporal or spiritual) was the only thing we had to do, and incited always by precept and example to do it well. An inflexible element of authority surrounded us all. We felt from the first (a useful thing) that our own wish had often nothing to say in the matter" (44).

In such an environment, Thomas Carlyle formed values and attitudes that lasted throughout his life. We hear little of lighthearted child's play. His boyhood energies were bent to the doctrines of work and faith by parents whose highest hope was that he might grow up to become a minister of the faith that they professed.

## II  *Education*

In keeping with their hopes to see him enter the ministry, Thomas' parents eagerly sought for evidence of their son's capability and rejoiced to discover him quick of mind and eager to learn. Recalling these years in later life, Thomas writes:

"I remember, perhaps in my fifth year, his teaching me arithmetical things, especially how to divide (my letters taught me by my mother, I have no recollection of whatever; of reading scarcely any). He said, This is the divider (divisor); this etc; and gave me a quite clear notion how to do it. My mother said I would forget it all; to which he answered, "Not so much as they that have never learnt it." Five years or so after he said to me once, "Tom, I do not grudge thy schooling, when thy uncle Frank owns thee a better arithmetician than himself." (46)

James was as good as his word, for in May 1806, when Thomas was ten years old, he walked to the village of Annan to enroll his son in the academy because instruction was reputed to be superior there. Carlyle's stay at the Annan Academy was successful but unhappy, if we are to accept Carlyle's own statement on the matter.[2] Just what caused his unhappiness at school is not entirely clear. His biographer, J. A. Froude, describes him at this period as "shy and thoughtful," but also of a "hot temper." Quite possibly, however, he was already isolated from his peers by character traits taught him at home. Serious and overly sensitive, he could not participate whole-heartedly in boyish activities and was treated as an outcast by his schoolmates. Despite his misery at Annan, which appears to be one source of his lifetime prejudice for scholars, Thomas learned enough to satisfy his teachers' expectations and to justify his parents' plans to send him to Edinburgh to enroll in the university.

In November of 1809, when Thomas was approaching his fourteenth year, he was sent to Edinburgh on foot in the company of Tom Smail, an older boy already in attendance at the university. The two boys, accompanied through the village by Thomas' parents, set out on a frosty morning for Edinburgh, which is just under one hundred miles from Ecclefechan. They traveled with light packs, walking about twenty miles a day, sleeping nights in inns or farms along the way. When they arrived at Edinburgh, they were welcomed by no officials and expected by none. They found their own lodgings and made their own arrangements for board. Most of the students had little money beyond their fees, and Carlyle was no exception. His parents sent him oatmeal, butter, and occasionally potatoes or cheese by carrier, and he in turn sent his clothing home to be washed and repaired.

He alone was responsible for his matriculation in the university and for his selection of lectures. Personal guidance in a student's studies depended upon the whims of the professor. Books were not plentiful and texts almost nonexistent. What little social life was available to the student of limited financial means did not attract

Carlyle, and he became increasingly lonely and discouraged. His family, however, watched his progress and eagerly awaited his entrance into the ministry.

At this time, Edinburgh University was in the sunset of its eighteenth century greatness. Its lectures still represented the rationalistic views of Locke and Hume, but the vitality of earlier years was absent. During Carlyle's residence at Edinburgh, reaction against the views of Hume and the Scottish realists was just beginning, but Carlyle found no professor speaking with the fiery apocalyptic zeal that his own spirits demanded. Gradually, his dissatisfaction with philosophy and theology increased, and he devoted more and more of this time to the field of mathematics, where he could move with certainty and conviction.

His personal life, meanwhile, was as discouraging to him as his intellectual progress. He was repelled by the activities of his fellow students at Edinburgh, just as he had been repelled by the boyish pranks and rough play of his schoolmates at Annan. As time passed, however, he found a small circle of congenial friends and correspondents who, to judge from their letters, were just as idealistic as Carlyle himself. Nevertheless, Carlyle's dissatisfaction with his college years is clearly expressed in a passage found in his occasionally autobiographical *Sartor Resartus:* "Besides all this we boasted ourselves a Rational University in the highest degree hostile to Mysticism; thus was the young vacant mind furnished with much talk about the Progress of the Species, Dark Ages, Prejudice, and the like; so that all were quickly blown out into a state of windy argumentativeness; whereby the better sort had soon to end in sick, impotent Scepticism; the worser sort explode (crepiren) in finished self-conceit, and to all spiritual intents become dead."[3] In spite of his growing alienation, Carlyle continued to attend Edinburgh, finishing his college course in 1814 at the age of nineteen.

## III  *Teaching*

He was now faced with a momentous problem. The option to enter the ministry was still open to him. He could attend lectures in the divinity hall at the university for four years or enter himself as a rural divinity student, in which case he must return every twelve months to deliver a sermon and to respond to the inquiries of the faculty. The growing uncertainty of his convictions and his continued need for financial support led him to the latter option. Hearing of a vacancy in mathematics at Annan school, he applied for the post; and when the position was offered him, he accepted it, thus beginning the most difficult period of his life.

In one sense, returning to Annan Academy after four years at Edinburgh was returning home to familiar boyhood haunts and faces. In another sense, it was returning to a school associated with boyhood unhappiness. Had it not been for the salary of £70 a year, Carlyle might not have accepted the appointment. Later, he wrote in his *Reminiscences,* "I was abundantly lonesome, uncomfortable and out of place there." (p. 72) He confessed that he made little effort to meet people in the community. The teaching became more and more disagreeable, and he grew to hate it, too. Here, as before, we find Carlyle unhappy and alienated, or nearly so, from society. He isolated himself in reading. He read always with an eye open to moral considerations, but shut to whatever was simply literary. During the winter, he continued to study Hume, although he was convinced of his *"prejudice* in *favour* of infidelity."[4] By the end of the year, December 11, 1815, Carlyle was busily engaged in writing his second exegesis for presentation to the divinity school at Edinburgh. Confiding his doubts to his friend Mitchell he wrote, "You will ask me, why, since I have almost come to a determination about my fitness for the study of Divinity, why all this mighty stir—why this ado—about 'delivering' a thesis—that in the mind's eye seems vile, and in the nostril smells horrible?" (*Early Letters,* 26). Still, he made the journey to Edinburgh during the Christmas holidays and again satisfied the faculty of his progress despite his growing doubts, but it was his last attempt to fit into the role of the minister. He had written his presentation in Latin on the question *"Num detur religio naturalis?"* Although he prepared no more exegeses and abandoned the ministry, he had discovered the question to which he devoted a large part of his life. In July 1816, as he approached the age of twenty-one, he was offered a better teaching position at Kirkcaldy that led to two of the most fateful associations of his life: his friendship with Edward Irving, and acquaintance with Margaret Gordon, his first love.

Carlyle's appointment to a teaching post at Kirkcaldy marks the beginning of his maturity. Edward Irving, who had established a reputation for brilliance at Edinburgh, was the principal master there. His continued success as a teacher at Kirkcaldy was achieved in the opinion of some citizens at the cost of overly severe methods. Carlyle's preferment was the result of efforts of townspeople who wished to hire a teacher less inclined to severity than Irving. A competitive arrangement might be expected to produce animosity between the two young men, but in this instance it did not. Irving and Carlyle became close friends. When Carlyle visited Kirkcaldy in August 1816, Irving did all he could to make his competitor welcome. In addition to his assurances of friendship, he put Carlyle up at his lodging for several nights, introduced him to friends, freely loaned him books from his library, took long walks with him, and seriously discussed issues uppermost in Carlyle's mind. Carlyle remembered this period as brightened by the "Blessed conquest of a friend in this world!" (*Reminiscences*, p. 80). Needing the encouragement and security that a confidant could give him, he remembered Irving's friendship with gratitude throughout his life.

Irving's friendship did not modify Carlyle's character. In spite of his efforts, Carlyle's sense of isolation persisted. In a letter to his mother, March 17, 1817, he wrote, "I have little intercourse with the natives here; yet there is no dryness between us. We are always happy to meet and happy to part; but their society is not very valuable to me, and my books are friends that never fail me."[5] Carlyle was saying that he has meager social life; and, moreover, that he prefers his isolation. But he was also assuring his mother that he has not forgotten the family doctrine of work.

It was not his preference to do entirely without human involvement, even though he found it emotionally exhausting. A notable instance of his personal need can be found in his continuing correspondence with Robert Mitchell, a fellow divinity student to whom he freely communicated his thoughts and concerns. Writing from Kirkcaldy February 16, 1818, he shows his situation to be unchanged: "I continue to teach (that I may subsist thereby), with about as much satisfaction as I should beat hemp, if such were my vocation. Excepting one or two individuals I have little society that I value very highly, but books are a ready and effective resource . . . . Before leaving this subject (theology) I wish to ask how your theological studies are advancing . . . ? I doubt my career 'in the above line' has come to a close" (*Early Letters*, 67 - 68). The ministry was no longer a real option, and teaching was rapidly becoming unbearable.

For a time he was fascinated by Margaret Gordon, whom he met at the home of Reverend J. Martin, the father of Irving's fiancé. The degree of Carlyle's emotional involvement with Miss Gordon has been equated with the passionate treatment of Blumine in *Sar-*

*tor Resartus,* where the relationship between Teufelsdröckh and Blumine suggests a dramatized version of Carlyle's feelings for Miss Gordon.

## IV   *Uncertainties*

By the fall of 1818, both Carlyle and Irving had decided to quit teaching. Irving remained constant to the ministry, but Carlyle was only certain of what he could not do. Early in November 1818, he informed Robert Mitchell that he had resigned his position. "Lucian (the Voltaire of antiquity)," he wrote, "has left his opinion, in writing, that when the Gods have determined to render a man ridiculously miserable, they make a schoolmaster of him; . . ." (84 - 85). He planned to go to Edinburgh for the winter, but could not decide upon a course of action beyond that. He thought of writing for booksellers and of studying for the law or for civil engineering. By the end of November, he was in Edinburgh without prospects and increasingly without hope. He tutored some, read widely, studied law and foreign languages, but made no real progress in deciding what to do with his life. His mother had not yet abandoned her hope that he could enter the ministry. "Do make religion your great study, Tom"; she wrote in April 1819, "if you repent it, I will bear the blame forever" (111). Carlyle could not dispell her hopes, but neither could he follow her wishes. Burdened with doubts, worried by finances, he withdrew to his books.

From May to November 1819, Carlyle was at home in Mainhill. His mother treated him as a patient, catering as well as she could to his moodiness and sensitivity to noise; and in the fall he returned to Edinburgh to the study of law. By March 1820, however, he had given it up; and on June 28, 1820, Margaret Gordon wrote, breaking off their friendship, "And now, my dear Friend, a long, long adieu. One advice, and as a parting one, consider—value it. *Cultivate the milder disposition of your heart, subdue the more extravagant* visions of the brain . . . . *Genius* will render you *great.* May *virtue* render you *beloved*! . . . I give you not my address, because I dare not promise to see you."[6] The loss of Margaret's friendship has been exaggerated by Carlyle's biographers because it marked the beginning of Carlyle's darkest period. He was working at biographies for inclusion in Professor Brewster's *Edinburgh Encyclopaedia,* but his lack of certain prospects seemed to have affected his health. His complaints were consistent and constant.

Work and piety, the doctrines taught him in his youth, seemed to be impossible achievements. Writing to his friend Mitchell in March 1821, he summarized his activities. "I meant to give you my history for the bygone months. It is easily done. I have had the most miserable health—was in a low fever for two weeks lately, meditating to come home, and actually did elope to Fife; and during all the winter I have had such delightful companions to interrupt my long solitudes, such intellectual, high-spirited men you have no idea of. My progress has been proportionable . . . . I have tried about twenty plans this winter in the way of authorship; they have all failed; . . ." (*Early Letters*, 160).

Discovering him in his black mood, late in May, Irving took him on a walking trip to Haddington in East Lothian, where he was delighted with Jane Welsh, earlier a student of Irving. Early in June, Carlyle reported to his brother Alexander that, though still ill, he was "happy as a lark in May" (*Early Letters*, 169). His correspondence with Miss Welsh dated from the time of this visit. He had sent her books to read and an elaborately coy letter of instructions and professions of admiration. When Jane Welsh returned the books with her compliments to Mr. "Carslile," he was crestfallen but still determined to enlarge his acquaintance. From this time until his marriage to Jane Welsh, Carlyle's complaints about his inability to work became more strident, and his reports of ill health became more constant. Froude stated that in June 1821, when Carlyle was twenty-six, the conversion experience described in *Sartor Resartus* occurred on Leith Walk, Edinburgh, but Carlyle's published correspondence gives no direct evidence to the exact time of it. The crescendo of his complaints rose steadily and became more colorful between 1821 and his marriage in 1826. By the end of 1823 he was either growing exceedingly skillful in expressing his misery or as desperate as ever he had been. "Hopeful youth Mr. C! Another year or two and it will do; another year or two and thou wilt *wholly* be the *caput mortum* of thy former self, a creature ignorant, stupid, peevish, disappointed, brokenhearted; the veriest wretch upon the surface of the globe. My curse seems deeper and blacker than that of any man: to be immured in a rotten carcass, every avenue of which is changed into an inlet of pain; till my intellect is obscured and weakened, and my head and heart are alike desolate and dark."[7]

David A. Wilson placed the Leith Walk incident in the summer of 1822, but the later date does little to explain Carlyle's complaints, which continued undiminished for several years. Even Carlyle, however, regarded the incident as a turning point in his life. He wrote of it in 1866, asserting, "Nothing in *Sartor* thereabouts is *fact* (symbolic *myth* all) except that of the 'incident in the Rue St. Thomas de l'Enfer,'—which happened quite literally to myself in Leith Walk, during those three weeks of total sleeplessness, in which almost my one solace was that of a daily bathe on the sands between Leith and Portobello."[8] We must come to the conclusion that the incident, though marking the end of one development, did not of itself solve Carlyle's problems.

Whatever the date of the Leith Walk experience, Carlyle's conversion was not completed until he was able to address himself to work with whole-hearted confidence and satisfaction. It was four years since Irving visited him in Edinburgh and took him on a walking visit to Haddington and Miss Welsh. After a long and wordy courtship—they wrote many romantically idealistic letters to one another—they were married in October 1826. But Carlyle's marriage is not the key to the resolution of his anxieties. During the period between 1821 and his marriage, he finished his preparations and turned toward his life's work.

His friend Irving, who was enjoying popularity as a preacher, recommended Carlyle as a tutor for the sons of Mr. Charles Buller, a retired Anglo-Indian, and Carlyle served in that post for two years. The salary of £200 a year freed Carlyle from financial worries. He bought books, sent presents home, and helped pay the cost of his brother's education. Even more important was the completion of his hack writing. The work for the *Edinburgh Encyclopaedia* was in the past. His translation of Legendre's mathematics was published in the spring of 1822. While tutoring the Buller boys, he discovered German literature. He began a life of the poet Schiller, which was published in the *London Magazine* in 1823, and the translation of Göethe's *Wilhelm Meister*.

He left the Buller position in 1824, and after a trip to Paris of twelve days and a period in London and Edinburgh, he went to Hoddam Hill near his parents' farm and settled down, reading and translating German writers. This study resolved his remaining anxiety: how to believe in God in his time. His soul crisis ended in the peace of Hoddam Hill.

My translation (German Romance) went steadily on . . . Internally, too, there were far higher things going on; a grand and ever joyful victory getting itself achieved at last! The final chaining down trampling home "for good," home into their caves for ever of all my spiritual dragons, which had wrought me such woe, and for a decade past had made my life black and bitter. This year 1826 saw the end of all that, with such a feeling on my part as may be fancied. I found it to be essentially what the Methodist people call their "conversion," the deliverance of their souls from the Devil and the pit; . . . This "holy joy," of which I kept silence, lasted sensibly in me for several years in blessed counterpoise to sufferings and discouragements enough; nor has it proved what I can call fallacious at any time since. My "spiritual dragons," thank heaven, do still remain strictly in their caves, forgotten and dead, which is indeed a conquest, and the beginning of conquests. [9]

Carlyle was nearing the end of his uncertainties, but not the end of his difficulties. He had discovered how to maintain his belief in God, but he had not discovered what to do.

## V  *Marriage*

Bright and willful, Jane Welsh had developed a schoolgirl love for Edward Irving, who had been her teacher at Kirkcaldy; but Irving had earlier entered into a long-standing agreement with Isabelle Martin, the daughter of a minister there. Whatever his feelings in the matter, Irving remained true to his promise to Isabelle. When he introduced Carlyle to Jane in 1821, he had little reason to suspect that he had made a match; however, the two were immediately fascinated by one another.

In the region of Kirkcaldy, Jane Welsh was an heiress. Her father, a doctor who died in the fall of 1819 from an infection passed on by a patient, had willed his wealth and property to his daughter. Mrs. Welsh and Jane lived together in comfort on Jane's inheritance, though it was but £200 a year; and Jane was locally regarded as a resident Portia, her home in Haddington as Belmont. Thus, the intrusion of the serious and penniless Mr. Carlyle brought to the surface issues concerning Mrs. Welsh's comfort and happiness once her daughter married.

From the mother's point of view Jane could hardly do worse than develop an attachment to Carlyle, who possessed in her eyes little of the economic security she required and few of the social graces she was accustomed to. He was dour, opinionated, and clumsy. His future was clouded with doubt. Haddington and environs agreed with Mrs. Welsh. Carlyle was no catch for their heiress.

But the opinions of Mrs. Welsh and the Haddington community did little to discourage Carlyle and even less, perhaps, to discourage Jane, who was used to having her own way. Still, the romance undoubtedly suffered because of Carlyle's inability to find a steady outlet for his energies. He had closed the door on religion and teaching. He was nearing the end of his tolerance for literary hackwork. He had resigned himself to ill health, which stood in the way of his literary efforts. Furthermore, his translations of the works of strange and unknown German romantic writers opened him to as much suspicion as recognition.

Thus the progress of the romance with Jane Welsh was beset with difficulties. Carlyle would not be a part of a household that included Mrs. Welsh, though he was perfectly willing to include his own family. He could not accept the social activities of Mrs. Welsh, who could not do without them, because he needed uninterrupted quiet for his reading and writing. On her part, Jane would not abandon her mother, with whom she was on the best of terms. In spite of her objections to the match, Mrs. Welsh played the role of accomodation, leasing and helping to furnish a house in 21 Comley Bank in the northwestern suburbs of Edinburgh. They were married October 17, 1826, in her grandfather's house at Templand, by the parish minister and arrived at Comley Bank that night.

Carlyle had written "Schiller," translated *Wilhelm Meister* from the German, prepared articles for the *Edinburgh Encyclopaedia*, and entered the reviews, but he was not yet finished with his apprenticeship.

### CHAPTER 3

# The Critical Essays

## I  The Development of the Metaphor

CARLYLE's ill health was certainly related to the problems he had with plans for marriage and to anxieties concerning
a profession, but all his perplexities were more closely tied to the
problems he had with point of view than with anything else. A
paradox of enormous significance blocked his way to any clear action. Reared in a pious family that placed its emphasis upon a code
of behavior intended to fulfill the demands of divine order, Carlyle
lived in a time in which society was engaged in a historic dispute
with the codes and institutions that supported it. He was caught in
the struggle between human freedom and social order. To embrace
the major movements of his time, he must reject his early training
and those who administered it. To stand firm with his family and
those he loved, he must reject his times. For all its apparent
simplicity, this paradox stood foremost in both his thoughts and
feelings.

Had not a belief in a divinely ordered universe played a large
part in his training, Carlyle might have managed to follow the tradition of blind faith: work and be silent. But after his experience with
rationalism at the University of Edinburgh, he could neither return
to the life his father followed nor accept the ministry that had been
his reason for leaving home. Once aware of the vast social revolution that surged around him, he could never after join it or avoid it.

His resolution of the paradox—a metaphor fully presented in *Sartor Resartus*—perceives matter as the embodiment of spirit. To view
human activities as the expression of mankind's spiritual condition
neatly resolved the paradox that plagued Carlyle by giving him the
means to see contemporary events always in a moral context. Thus,
he could reject both the "atheistic" reason of the eighteenth century and the romantic excesses of the nineteenth century as phases

of spiritual malaise. He could applaud the idealism of contemporary romantics while condemning their self-centeredness. He could evaluate all social developments without becoming an expert of any. And he could accomplish all this in the knowledge that he had remained true to his convictions. Because forms and institutions were judged by moral criteria, he rejected the religious movements of his day on the same grounds that he rejected rationalism. He saw the history of people, nations, and cultures as the outward expressions of a deeper spiritual condition. His metaphor was clear, but the authentic reading of people and their histories required further development.

Men who failed to see beyond the physical appearance of the universe became the disbelievers, impoverished in soul and brutalized in body. Those who could see the spirit beyond the material surfaces of things he explored throughout his literary career. They are the heroes of his works, and in all of them he found elements of his own experience. The man marked for distinction experiences rising frustrations in health or in occupation. Frustrations deepen into doubts about the nature of self and the meaning of life. Unresolved doubts produce the rising anxiety and self-centeredness that force the subject into the deepest shadow of melancholy and disbelief. This is the "soul crisis" through which the hero passes to the death of self. In the very depth of disbelief, he abandons self-concern and affirms the eternal, unchanging, underlying realities of the spiritual universe.

Carlyle's notion of individual development required renunciation of self, which he often expressed as *selbst-tödtung* or *entsagen*. Although the reliability of the hero's vision was improved by the loss of self-interest, the original paradox deepened. While affirming the spiritual nature of man, he rejected the self-conscious creature of social, political, and moral convention. While recognizing man's reliance upon necessities, he would have man indifferent to them. While despising well-fed pomposity, he also despised the beggar who will steal to allay his hunger. Underlying all his writing, the grim paradox of the human condition remained. Only a society of heroes can happily starve while they feed upon the glory of a divine but meatless program. Man may merge with idea, but he does so at great risk. The unselfconscious man can exist only in utopia or in a rigidly structured society.

At the time of his marriage in 1826, however, Carlyle believed that he had solved his personal crisis. He had discovered men with whom he sympathized in German literature, and he was ready to publish his discoveries to the world. The periodical review offered an opportunity for publication to the unknown writer, and Carlyle wrote a great many of his early essays for the *Edinburgh Review*, whose editor, Francis Jeffery, had befriended him. Though writing on a great variety of topics, he made use of a small number of ideas repeatedly: matter is a metaphor of spirit; man has turned away from truth and belief to self-centeredness and doubt; histories of people and nations are dramas of spiritual health or spiritual illness; the life of the hero is the drama of the "soul crisis" resolved in faith. Topics as dissimilar as "Burns" and "Chartism" served as points of departure for the expression of the insights that constantly dominated his thinking.

Carlyle did not require evidence of all stages of the "soul crisis" and its resolution. On occasion, he inferred the entire process from the end result. In the essay entitled "Göethe," for example, spiritual conflict is not discussed. Even so, he attributed Göethe's later serenity to the successful outcome of an earlier period of spiritual torment.

For Göethe has not only suffered and mourned in bitter agony under the spiritual perplexities of his time; but he has also mastered these, he is above them, and has shown others how to rise above them. At one time, we found him in darkness, and now he is in light; he was once an Unbeliever, and now he is a Believer; and he believes, moreover, not by denying his unbelief, but by following it out; not by stopping short, still less turning back, in his inquiries, but by resolutely prosecuting them.[1]

The soul crisis can be resolved only by pursuing doubts to a point at which concern for self disappears and the will of God takes its place.

Although the soul crisis may follow religious doubt, it sometimes results from any severe shock to personal will. In the case of Novalis, the cause is the loss of his beloved Sophie. "For spirits like Novalis, earthly fortune is in no instance so sweet and smooth, that it does not by and by teach the great doctrine of *Entsagen*, of 'Renunciation' " (*Essays*, II, 15). If the spiritual struggle of his hero is not apparent, Carlyle will infer it from simple piety, unusual accomplishments, or a serene life, as in the case of Schiller in whose life "the completeness of the victory hides from us the magnitude of the struggle" (II, 193).

The ordinary mortal did not emerge from his soul crisis with complete victory or with victory at all. At times he became disheartened by the struggle and thus failed to attain the selflessness that he identified as characteristic of the greatest men. Burns, unlike Göethe, had not fought on to victory; therefore, he lacked a religious principle whereon he might base his life. "He lives in darkness and in shadow of doubt, his Religion, at best, is an anxious wish; like that of Rabelais, 'a great Perhaps' " (I, 313). Lacking belief, Burns was unable to fulfill the promise of his sincerity and love of truth. As Voltaire, who also failed because he could not achieve faith, Burns was unable to see the world as a metaphor of divine will. Voltaire's failure, however, is more spectacular than the poet's. "Accordingly, he [Voltaire] sees but a little way into Nature; the mighty All, in its beauty, and infinite mysterious grandeur, humbling the small *Me* into nothingness, has never even for moments been revealed to him; only this or that other atom of it, and the differences and discrepancies of these two, has he looked into and noted down. . . . 'The Divine Idea, that which lies at the bottom of Appearance,' was never more invisible to any man" (I, 425). Voltaire blindly made the multitude his master and became "simply a Man of the World, such as Paris and the eighteenth century produced and approved of: a polite, attractive, most cultivated, but essentially self-interested man . . ." (I, 425). Carlyle did not respect talent and intelligence apart from its service to what he saw as divine will.

Prophets and prophet-poets are the heroes of the early essays. These are the men who, as Werner, Göethe, and Novalis, contend with soul crisis successfully and emerge from their experience with visions of heavenly order and beauty. On occasion, however, Carlyle wrote about men who did not achieve the "everlasting yea." His essay on Burns is perhaps the leading example of the failure to achieve the ideal reached by Göethe or Novalis. After 1832, he turned to men of action for his topics, though he never gave them his fullest endorsement. Mirabeau and Francia are neither poets nor prophets, but they are more satisfactory than Voltaire and Diderot, who "looked upwards for the *Divine Eye*, and beheld only the black, bottomless, glaring *Death's Eye-socket* . . ." (III, 230).

## II   *The Later Essays*

Carlyle never doubted the superiority of the inspired poet-hero or prophet-hero; but, as time passed, he became less confident that one might appear who would lead mankind to a better life. Thus by

1843, when "Dr. Francia" appeared, he had resigned himself to the use of practical heroes for the presentations of his message. Dr. Francia, dictator of Paraguay from 1814 to 1840, far from being an ideal hero, was nevertheless a man devoted to orderly government. He was a hero of sorts in Carlyle's eyes, though Carlyle apologized for the fact that Francia was not more clearly inspired by God. "Poor Francia," he writes, "his light was but a very sulphurous, meagre, blue-burning one; but he irradiated Paraguay with it (as our Professor says) the best he could" (IV, 306).

Throughout the biographical essays, Carlyle's theme remains unchanged. Every life is revelation. But as time passed, more of Carlyle's heroes were men of action, and fewer of them were men of ideas. Carlyle knew that his heroes were no longer idealists. He expressed his regret often that they were no better than they were. He was trapped by his own convictions. Given his belief that human action revealed spiritual condition and his equally strong faith in divine intervention in the affairs of men, he found himself justifying people and actions that could not have been attractive in and of themselves. Carlyle must, finally, approve of the strong trends of his age or change the nature of his faith. A divinity who did not interact with the world he created placed unacceptable limitations on his powers. Thus, the developments of the nineteenth century confirmed Carlyle's suspicion that his age was not destined for high spiritual development. Meanwhile, Carlyle drifted steadily toward the support of whatever "maker's of order" he could find. Because divine will could not be frustrated, the half-heroes of politics and industry must have the approval of God. The Dr. Francias cannot rise even to the heights of half-hero, but they still prevail over their allotment of chaos.

## III    The Social Order

Carlyle's essays on social problems are often more astonishing than those on individuals. Indeed, the statements he makes in his social essays are responsible for his present reputation as an outright fascist.[2] The opinions expressed in "Signs of the Times," "Characteristics," "Chartism," "Dr. Francia," "The Nigger Question," and "Shooting Niagara: and After," whether met in context or out, affront the sensibilities of readers. In "Chartism" he wrote: "The time has come when the Irish population must either be improved a little, or else exterminated" (IV, 139). In the same essay he wrote, "How *can-do*, if we will well interpret it, unites itself with *shall-do* among mortals; how strength acts ever as the right-arm of justice; how might and right, so frightfully discrepant at first, are ever in the long-run one and the same,—is a cheering consideration" (147). He also wrote, "If precisely the Wisest Man were at the top of society, and the next-wisest next, and so on till we reached the Demerara Nigger (from which downwards, through the horse, etc., there is no question hitherto), then were this a perfect world, the extreme *maximum* of wisdom produced in it" (361). Among the many social pronouncements to be found in nineteenth century literature, those uttered by Thomas Carlyle are the most outrageous.

But Carlyle's basic assumptions are different from those of most commentators. He believed that God is active in the arena of human activities, and he believed that divine participation manifested itself through the authority and power it bestowed upon its chosen.

Recognized or not recognized, a man *has* his superiors, a regular hierarchy above him; extending up, degree above degree, to Heaven itself and God the Maker, who made His world not for anarchy but for rule and order! It is not a light matter when the just man can recognize in the powers set over him no longer anything that is divine; when resistance against such becomes a deeper law of order than obedience to them; when the just man sees himself in the tragical position of a stirrer-up of strife! (189)

His views never changed. They are the outgrowths of his deepest convictions concerning the nature of the universe.

As early as 1829, in "Signs of the Times," he characterized his age as atheistic and materialistic, denounced its emphasis on logic and mechanics, and lamented what he saw as the passing of faith, loyalty, and patriotism. "Characteristics," published in 1831, makes essentially the same points: "The healthy Understanding, we should say, is not the Logical, argumentative, but the Intuitive; for the end of Understanding is not to prove and find reasons, but to know and believe" (III, 5). He condemned the self-consciousness of society as something worse than error. "Self-contemplation, . . . is infallibly the symptom of disease, be it or be it not the sign of cure" (7). During the decade of the 1830s, Carlyle abandoned the celebration of the transcendental and demanded order in life and government. He synthesized the ideas of German philosophy with his own deep faith in an imminent God. Henceforth, he rarely wrote of poetry or aesthetics, but searched history and contemporary events for illustrations of his conviction that the universe is determined and that God, through nature and history, is the great determiner. Thus, in 1843, he supported the severe and arbitrary actions taken by Dr. Francia, the South American dictator; and in 1849, in "The Nigger Question," he expressed his convictions even more pointedly. "I say, if a Black gentleman is born to be a servant, and, in fact, is useful in God's creation only as a servant, then let him hire not by the month, but by a very much longer term" (IV, 368). Such views permit no sympathy for the democratic movements of the nineteenth century.

## IV   *The* Latter-Day Pamphlets

In 1850, Carlyle published eight essays collected under the title *Latter-Day Pamphlets.*[3] These essays, from first to last, make explicit the shapeless ideas of his early works but they do not reveal any basic changes in his convictions. Having abandoned hope for the conversion of society, he now spoke of crises, revolutions, and trials in the spirit of Jeremiah."God is great," he wrote,"and when a scandal is to end, brings some devoted man to take charge of it in hope, not in despair" (*LDP*, 3)! Although he still looked to the hero for salvation, the hero is no longer a poet. His age, he now believes, requires a warrior-king who can read the will of God. "A divine message, or eternal regulation of the Universe, there verily is, in regard to every conceivable procedure and affair of man: Faithfully following this, said procedure or affair will prosper, and have the Whole Universe to second it, and carry it, across the fluctuating contradictions, towards a victorious goal; not following this, disregarding this, destruction and wreck are certain for every affair" (17). Thus, the hope of the world lies in discovering "the true 'commander' and king; he who knows for himself the divine Appointments of this Universe, the Eternal Laws ordained by God the Maker, in conforming to which lies victory and felicity, in departing from which lies, and forever must lie, sorrow and defeat, for each and all of the Posterity of Adam in every time and every place" (32 - 33). Democracy, which determines right by popular vote, he saw as being a hopeless and even Godless affair. "Alas, on this side of the Atlantic and on that, Democracy, we apprehend, is forever impossible! . . . The Universe itself is a Monarchy and Hierarchy; large liberty of 'voting' there, all manner of choice, utmost free-will, but with conditions inexorable and immeasurable annexed to every exercise of the same. A most free commonwealth of 'voters'; but with Eternal Justice to preside over it, Eternal Justice enforced by Almighty Power" (21 - 22)! If the choice of the voter was the choice of God, all was well; but if the choice of the voter reflected his will only, it could never prevail.

Carlyle's ideas have some important implications. If the divine spirit is as closely involved in human history as Carlyle believed, philanthropic efforts may be little more than attempts to frustrate the will of God. "It seems not to have struck these good men that no world, or thing here below, ever fell into misery, without having first fallen into folly, into sin against the Supreme Ruler of it, by adopting as a law of conduct what was not a law, but the reverse of one; and that, till its folly, till its sin be cast out of it, there is not the smallest hope of its misery going, — that not for all the charity and rose-water in the world will its misery try to go till then" (49)! This reasoning led Carlyle to condemn prison reform along with doles and charities. Citizens who were stupid, idle, or criminal received little aid or comfort at the hands of Thomas Carlyle. He seems to be quite prepared to dispatch hopeless cases.

They are Adam's children,—alas yes, I well remember that, and never shall forget it; hence this rage and sorrow. But they have gone over to the dragons; they have quitted the Father's house, and set-up with the Old Serpent: till they return how can they be brothers? They are enemies, deadly to themselves and to me and to you, till then; till then, while hope yet lasts, I will treat them as brothers fallen insane;—when hope has ended, with tears grown sacred and wrath grown sacred, I will cut them off in the name of God! (66)

His final judgement for the idle is servitude and for the criminal is death.

In sharp contrast, the bright and the talented are the children of God. By Carlyle's definition, they can do no wrong.

True nevertheless it forever remains that Intellect is the real object of reverence and of devout prayer, and zealous wish and pursuit, among the sons of men; and even, well understood, the one object. It is the Inspiration of the Almighty that giveth men understanding. For it must be repeated . . . That a man of Intellect, of real and not sham Intellect, is by the nature of it likewise inevitably a man of nobleness, a man of courage, rectitude, pious strength; who even *because* he is and has been loyal to the

Laws of this Universe, is initiated into *discernment* of the same; to this hour a Missioned of Heaven . . . (106 - 107).

All responsibility for government belongs in the hands of this divinely chosen, intellectually elite class. "These are appointed, by the true eternal 'divine right' which will never become obsolete, to be your governors and administrators; and precisely as you employ them, or neglect to employ them will your State be favoured of Heaven or disfavoured" (130). Government by any other group is, Carlyle believes, "a curse and a sin . . . a Damned *lie* . . ." (140).

Government, safely in the hands of God's chosen rulers, will have absolute control of the individual. Idleness and unemployment will vanish from the face of the earth, for Carlyle anticipates the modern police state in its regimentation of labor. "Wise obedience and wise command, I forsee that the regimenting of Pauper Banditti into Soldiers of Industry is but the beginning of this blessed process, which will extend to the topmost heights of our Society; and, in the course of generations, make us all once more a Governed Commonwealth, and *Civitas Dei*, if it please God! . . . in the end, all kinds of Industry whatsoever, will be found capable of regimenting" (166). Although in 1867, in "Shooting Niagara: and After?," he predicts that democracy will have run its course, that the Christian religion "shall have deliquesced," and that there "shall be Free Trade, in all senses and to all degrees," he has not modified his convictions (*Essays*, V, 1 - 2). The great events of his day did not change his position on government, labor, or any social problem. He saw society on the Niagara River moving rapidly toward the falls and certain destruction. His only hope lay in the elite. He believed that the aristocracy of nature, which includes men of speculative and practical ability, and the aristocracy by title might unite to "make manifest to mankind that 'Reverence for God and for Man' is not yet extinct . . ." (29). And he asserts again that the ruler of the land "introduce wisely a universal system of Drill, not military only, but human in all kinds; so that no child or man born in *his* territory might miss the benefit of it" (42).

In his social utterances, Carlyle sets himself against the trends of his times at every opportunity. He views society as an organic thing that functions as naturally as the healthy human body if the right person or persons are in control. He believes that God's appointed leaders will have the strength and wisdom to make all parts of the social body function in good health, even if a few must be cut away in the process. The problems touched upon in the essays are, for the most part, the problems treated in greater detail in his book length works.

CHAPTER 4

# Views on the Nature and Function of Biography

### I    The "Seeing Eye"

HAVING found a point of view that reduced man and society to the manifestation of the divine spirit, Carlyle turned to the expression of it. Because his point of view allowed him to examine men and nations as evidence of spiritual health, he could satisfy the urgings of his conscience to preach and to prophesy without putting on the robes of the clergyman or the diction of the theologian. Because he believed that every life exhibits the struggle between the divine spirit and elemental chaos, he turned to the writing of biographies of men and societies as his work in the world.[1]

He discussed biography in "On History," "Biography," "Boswell's Life of Johnson," and "Sir Walter Scott." These essays, amplified by his practice in writing, present an unusual view of biography and of the biographer. Biography is the struggle of the individual man to discover the will of God, and the biographer is the man who can identify this struggle and present it in a way in which it can be used to inform the reader of the will of God. In as much as it displays the resolution of the conflicts between order and chaos on spiritual, social, and personal levels, it must be written by the man who possesses the ability to discover the spiritual struggle in human life. Carlyle calls this ability "the seeing eye," but what he means is that the biographer must have the ability to recognize the visible world as a metaphor of the spirit and to accept its operations as holy revelation.

Conflict, taken as the struggle of man to learn the divine will, is the heart of his biographical method.

No man lives without jostling and being jostled; in all ways he has to *elbow* himself through the world, giving and receiving offence. His life is a battle, in so far as it is an entity at all. . . . his conflict is continual with the spirit of contradiction, that is without and within; with the evil spirit (or call it, with the weak, most necessitous, pitiable spirit), that is in others and in himself. His walk, like all walking (say the mechanicians), is a series of *falls*. To paint a man's life is to represent these things. (*Essays*, IV, 30)

Although Carlyle does not render his criteria concrete, the reader soon learns to tell the right side of the conflict. Order is divine; disorder is infernal. Work is godly; sloth is evil. Strength of mind or of body is holy, and weakness, if not quite evil, is lamentable. For Carlyle, the very facts of life are religion or lack of it. Thus, conflict is presented in *Sartor Resartus* by his hero's name. Diogenes Teufelsdröckh (Born-of-God Devil's-dung) embodies the paradoxical nature of human existence. Social chaos, representing the hand of God working retribution in the destructive force of revolution, is the theme of *The French Revolution.* Worship of the individual ordained as a special agent of God to resolve conflict on various levels of human action is the major concern of *Heroes and Hero-Worship.* *Past and Present* is a comparison of the resolution of conflict created by a hero like Abbot Samson with the disorder created by self-serving men like Plugson of Undershot and Sir Jabesh Windbag. The *Life of John Sterling* is the story of one man's struggle with the forces of chaos. *Frederick the Great* shows the order that can be attained by a nation that is governed by a strong man.

Carlyle's view of man and society arises from his conviction that God's intervention in the world of man on the side of order is accomplished through the hero. This doctrine accounts for Carlyle's attacks on political and social democracy as well as for his literary method. Without it, few, if any, of his works could have been written. Biography held a central position in his work because it could be extended to social proportions. "Social Life is the aggregate of all individual men's Lives who constitute society; History is the essence of innumerable Biographies" (II, 86). As an extension of biography, history, too, held its divine message secret until perceived by the "seeing eye" of the biographer. It, too, contained the hidden and immutable divine truth. "Let us search more and more into the Past; let all men explore it, as the true fountain of knowledge; by whose light alone, consciously or unconsciously employed, can the Present and the Future be interpreted or guessed at" (89). Throughout his life, he saw history as the struggle of a people to reduce infernal chaos to divine order.

For the Past is all holy to us; the Dead are all holy, even they that were base and wicked while alive. Their baseness and wickedness was not They, was but the heavy and unmanageable Environment that lay round them, with which they fought unprevailing: *they* (the ethereal god-given Force that dwelt in them and was their *Self)* have now shuffled-off that heavy environment, and are free and pure: their life-long Battle, go how it might, is all ended, with many wounds or with fewer; they have been recalled from it, and the once harsh-jarring battlefield has become a silent awe-inspiring Golgotha, and *Gottesacker* (Field of God)! (III, 55 - 56)

Such views, strange though they may sound to the contemporary reader, are keys to the understanding of Carlyle's writing. His point of view controls the "seeing eye" that discerns a cosmic struggle between good and evil in the factual details of his topic.

Thus, biographical writing was never just a literary effort for him. He believed that he was writing a gospel, or a portion of one. "For as the highest Gospel was a Biography, so is the Life of every good man still an indubitable Gospel, and preaches to the eye and heart and whole man, so that Devils even must believe and tremble, these gladdest tidings: 'Man is heaven-born'; . . ." (90). The literary quality of a biography is of secondary importance. Its chief purpose is to reveal God's will through the life of God's creature.

## II   *The "Loving Heart"*

Whereas the "seeing eye" accounts for the dramatic quality of his writing, the "loving heart" often contributes a lyrical quality to it. Carlyle celebrates the divine whenever he perceives it in the actions of men. When he writes of a hero thoroughly acceptable to his "seeing eye," his "loving heart" expresses its admiration in heightened diction and rhymical prose. Carlyle wrote in misery when he wrote of doubt; but when he perceived the work of God, he expressed himself in a way that was itself an act of worship. Throughout his life, he was happy only when at work on the expression of his great metaphor. When he was unable to express his conviction concerning the nature of the world, his misery returned. Convinced that the struggles of man are holy and that the hero expressed divine will through his life, he quite naturally became a worshipper of heroes. The "loving heart" as a principle of biography was also an act of worship.

Carlyle distinguished the ideal hero from the ordinary man whatever his status, and he preferred to write about the hero-prophet or the hero-poet who had attained peace and order. This hero must have attained to what Carlyle calls *entsagen*. *Entsagen*, renunciation of self, qualified a man as a worker of divine will and as a suitable subject for biography. But *entsagen*, he believed, was achieved through prolonged suffering. His heroes, therefore, suffered. "Samuel had whispered to himself: I too am 'one and somewhat.' False thoughts; that leave only misery behind! The fever-fire of ambition is too painfully extinguished (but not cured) in the frostbath of Poverty" (95). Johnson's failure to attain renunciation of self through suffering leads Carlyle to deny him the admiration he reserves for those who become "perfect through suffering." Even so, he has earned Carlyle's respect.

Lesser men may be used as the subject of biographies, but their lives are to be used as warnings, not as models. Carlyle used Johnson as an example of a good, if not heroic, subject for biography. He used Sir Walter Scott as an example of a man not well qualified because of his spiritual inadequacy. "Friends to precision of epithet will probably deny his title to the name 'great.' . . . His life was worldly; his ambitions were worldly. There is nothing spiritual in him; all is economical, material, of the earth earthy" (IV, 35). The "loving heart" may pity the imperfect man, but it worships the true hero.

Thus, the fact that Scott wrote many novels that amused a large public was not in itself sufficient cause to call him great. Measured by Carlyle's *entsagen*, he has been found wanting. "But so it was: in this nineteenth century, our highest literary man, who immeasurably beyond all others commanded the world's ear, had, as it were, no message whatever to deliver to the world; wished not the world to elevate itself, to amend itself, to do this or to do that, except simply pay him for the books he kept writing" (54). Shakespeare came under the same criticism. Both writers, Carlyle believed, wrote with no other intent than to amuse their audiences. He demanded a serious purpose of literature. "The candid judge will, in general, require that a speaker, in so extremely serious a Universe as this of ours, have something to speak about. In the heart of the speaker there ought to be some kind of gospel-tidings, burning till it be uttered; otherwise it were better for him that he altogether held his peace" (55). Carlyle's rigid attitude toward writing explains his negative judgements of many of his contemporaries who were literary men, first and foremost. Writing must have an elevating message or, at least, a moral orientation before he could consider it seriously. Writing novels without a moral point is lamentable in itself, but writing novels to "cover the walls of a stone house in Selkirkshire with nick-nacks, ancient armour and genealogical shields" (73) is an unforgiveable act. Scott's life is "one proof more that Fortune stands on a restless *globe;* that Ambition, literary, warlike, political, pecuniary, never yet profited any man" (84). Scott was a man of talent who had not perfected himself through suffering.

## III   *The Hero*

A moment's consideration reveals that Carlyle's biography shares characteristics with much writing from other periods. Given his concern for the spiritual quality of his subject, the result bears some comparison with the saints' lives of the middle ages. His emphasis on the ritualized development of his subject relates it to quest literature of almost any age. His spartanlike attention to duty and service calls to mind legends of the noble warrior. And his concern for the nature of the biographer himself reminds us of the romantics of his own age. A more general view of the biographies gives one a clear impression of Carlyle's artistry, for they are carefully tailored, not so much to their subjects as to Carlyle's dominant ideas. These are found in some of the world's great literature. The most important are those concerning the nature of the hero.

Carlyle's *entsagen* (renunciation of self) is a characteristic possessed by many literary heroes and by some historical ones. Roland's sacrificial stand comes to mind, as does Sir Philip Sidney's denial of water when mortally wounded so that another might have it. Lear is humbled, if not perfected, by suffering in Shakespeare's play. Shakespeare portrays Coriolanus's decision not to enter Rome as a spectacular renunciation of self. The martyrs Latimer and Ridley burned at the stake for their religious convictions without the slightest concern for self, according to reports. What distinguishes Carlyle's biographies from other literary creations is the synthesis he made of readily available materials.

Because biography in its modern form was just coming into being when Carlyle began to write, he had few models to draw upon. He knew Plutarch's *Lives* and had read Isaac Walton's lives and Roper's life of Sir Thomas More; but he found Boswell's *Life of Samuel Johnson* to be the best model for his purposes. He borrowed something from all of them. But *entsagen,* his most important doctrine, was readily at hand in the New Testament's depiction of the life of Christ. His "seeing eye" is little more than the practice of biblical exegesis applied to nonbiblical matter; and his "loving heart," though he attributed it to Boswell, is almost certainly the attitude of worship learned at his mother's knee.

What renders Carlyle's synthesis of these traditional materials striking is his style, which is always a matter of concern for the artist. Although his style, as pointed out elsewhere, is also a synthesis of influences, the point to be made in the context of Carlyle's biographical writing is that, except in the *Life of John Sterling*, he abandoned the conventions of writing held during his own time and developed a manner of writing that, he believed, spoke from the heart. It also drew commentary from friends and critics alike. The description of a selfless hero working the will of God written in unconventional prose by a dedicated worshipper of heroes has considerable dramatic appeal, if nothing else.

## IV  *The Biographer*

The biographer is nearly as important as the hero. To write successful biography, Carlyle believed, a biographer must be a worshipper of heroes. Carlyle used the character of James Boswell as an example of the ideal nature of the biographer. Boswell had an open, loving heart that compelled him to acknolwedge excellence where it existed. He demonstrated the lost art of discipleship, a reverence for divine wisdom, becoming thereby a practical witness to the high truth of hero worship. His *Life of Samuel Johnson* is a kind of heroic poem that proves that the heart sees farther than the head. "Boswell wrote a good Book," Carlyle believes, "because he had a heart and an eye oo discern Wisdom, and an utterance to render it forth; because of his free insight, his lively talent, above all, of his Love and childlike Openmindedness" (III, 76). The "loving heart" establishes a highly personal relationship between the biographer and his subject. It is the element that justifies his style and certifies his romanticism.

Carlyle was now ready for his life's work. He had developed a point of view. He had discovered how he might fulfill his need for worship in his work. His final task was to see that his work fulfilled his principles. "The biographer has this problem set before him; to delineate a likeness of the earthly pilgrimage of a man. He will compute well what profit is in it, and what disprofit; under which latter head this of offending any of his fellow creatures will surely not be forgotten. . . . But once taken up, the rule before all rules is to do *it*, not to do the ghost of it" (IV, 31). Although some of what he wrote was offensive enough, most of his writing adheres to the principles he established for biographical writing.

Carlyle gave to biography a spiritually didactic emphasis as great as it has ever had. Although he accepted the methods of eighteenth century biography in theory, he never really practiced them. He defined the aim of biography as the writing of true scripture. The principles that he set forth in his early essays exert vigorous influence upon all his works.

# CHAPTER 5

# Sartor Resartus

AT once the most difficult and the most read of Carlyle's works, *Sartor Resartus* is also the key to Carlyle's writing. It marks the emergence of his characteristic style, and it contains all the elements of his thought. Lacking the acerbity of much of his later writing, it is one of his most attractive works.

The book is difficult to summarize because of its associational method of development and because of its metaphorical presentation of subject. Throughout the book, the clothes metaphor is applied to all social, political, and personal customs, which are seen as the outward expression of underlying spiritual attitudes and convictions. Thus, the book is an attack on the materialism of its day, which is analogous to clothing valued not for its function but for itself.

## I  *Book I*

Despite the advanced state of culture, no book has been written on the philosophy of clothes. Perhaps the practical nature of England has proved to be unfavorable to the development of abstract thought; however, Germany has come to our aid with the arrival of a new book entitled *Clothes, Their Origin and Influence*, by Diogenes Teufelsdröckh, published by Stillschweigen and Co., Weissnichtwo, 1831. The English editor is perplexed how to present Professor Teufelsdröckh's meaning, but is aided by an unexpected letter from Herr Hofrath Heuschrecke, a friend of Teufelsdröckh, who promises biographical data on the author. This letter encourages the English editor, and the life and opinions of Herr Teufelsdröckh rapidly take shape.

Teufelsdröckh, a professor of things in general at the University of Weissnichtwo, is known there chiefly for his appearance at the local coffeehouse. He is a thinker of transcendental nature, little given to talk, who holds a lonely professorship, without students or lectures. He lives in the attic of the highest house in town, from where he can observe the entire city. There he is cared for by a redoubtable old lady named Liza who keeps his lodging in order. His only close acquaintance is Herr Heuschrecke. His book follows the transcendental practice of looking at all matter and material things as spiritual. His style is marred by circumlocutions, repetitions, and even jargon. The feelings expressed, however, exhibit love and pity under the rude, exterior style. Laughter for Teufelsdröckh is not frequent, but it is whole-hearted when it occurs. All in all his book is badly arranged, but the editor will attempt to bring order to it. Cause and effect thinking is abandoned as inadequate to express the philosophy of clothes. Teufelsdröckh reviews a variety of clothing and admits that, on the whole, man is a tool-using animal.

He discusses aprons as a defense of clothing, considers paper aprons worn by French cooks, and concludes that journalists are now the true kings and clergy. He returns to his subject in a discussion of ancient German costume and pauses to consider the costume of Bolivar's cavalry. He undertakes an explanation of the moral, political, and religious influence of clothes and asks the question, "Who am I; what is this me?" Space is but a mode of human sense, as is time. The me is the only reality. Nature is the visible garment of God. Man is a spirit bound to all men, and his clothes are the visible fact of his brotherhood. Underneath their clothing all men are alike. Man is hidden beneath his garment of flesh. God's presence is manifested to man's eyes and heart. Matter, however despicable, is the manifestation of the spirit. The thing visible or even the thing imagined is the clothing of the celestial invisible. The beginning of wisdom is to look on clothes till they become transparent and reveal the wonder of man, which is the basis of worship.

Science destroys wonder, and man without wonder is blind. Because all visible things are emblems, matter functions only to represent some idea, to body forth the spirit. As for man himself, his whole terrestrial life is but an emblem, a clothing of the divine. Even language is all metaphor. Man is the only object that interests man. The book concludes with the announcement that Herr Heuschrecke has sent the materials for a biography of Teufelsdröckh in six paper bags.

## II  *Book II*

Book Two is the life of Teufelsdröckh. He is a foundling given to the keeping of Andreas Futteral and his wife. His name Diogenes Teufelsdröckh is his earliest garment. Nothing can be discovered of his parents or of the man who brought him to the Futterals. He spends his early life in pastoral Entepfuhl. He learns his father's stories and discovers the larger world and the wonders of the seasons. He is forced to obey. He is taught the simple Christian faith of his foster parents. When the time comes, he is sent to school. He does not care for his rude classmates, and his instruction is poor. Eventually he goes to the university, which is the worst of all, outside England and Spain. It is a rational university, and he is overtaken with doubt. His condition is made less bearable by poverty. He meets Herr Towgood. He has difficulty finding what to do. He is invited to the Zahdarm's aesthetic tea, but he can find no work.

He gives up the profession of law and falls in love with a young lady named Blumine. His love grows, but she rejects him for a richer suitor. He falls into the abyss of self-pity and travels throughout the world. He will not love a second time. Seeing Herr Towgood and Blumine passing by in a carriage, his self-pity darkens. He becomes a wanderer, urged forward by despair.

His doubt darkens to unbelief. Still, he loves truth. The universe seems void of life, of purpose, of volition, even of hostility. It is a steam engine indifferently rolling on. On Rue Saint Thomas de L'Enfer he asks, "What *art* thou afraid of?" The Everlasting No said, "Behold thou art fatherless, outcast, and the universe is mine (the devil's)." He answers, "I am not thine, but free and forever hate thee (*Sartor Resartus*, 135). From this point Teufelsdröckh clutches the *not-me* as wholesome food and thinks about man's activity in law and government. He reads books. He discovers that great men are the inspired (speaking and acting) texts of that divine book of revelations. After much roasting, he has become calcined. He has reached the center of indifference.

He discovers the god-given mandate, "work thou in well doing." He looks out to nature, which he sees as the living garment of God. He discovers that the universe is not dead, but living and godlike. He concludes that he must pass from idle suffering to actual endeavouring. Only with renunciation (*entsagen*) can life begin. Love not pleasure, love God is the Everlasting Yea. Conviction must become action. The man is the spirit he works in; not what he does but what he becomes.

### III  *Book III*

The most remarkable incident in modern history is George Fox's making himself a suit of leather. Every stitch pricks into the heart of slavery and world worship. Church clothes are spun and woven by society. Every society is a church. Today our church clothes are out at the elbows.

Man is guided and commanded by symbols. The universe is a vast symbol of God. Man himself is a symbol of God. Everything he makes is but the visible record of invisible things. The highest of all symbols are those in which the artist or poet has risen into prophet. Our divinest symbol is Jesus of Nazareth.

Teufelsdröckh honors the craftsman and he who toils for the spiritual things. He considers society as good as extinct. The sacred symbols are empty. The church is fallen speechless and the state shrunken into a police office. Independence of all kinds is rebellion. The world is in a process of devastation and waste. Actually, society is not dead, but only weaving herself new clothing. She will rise Phoenixlike. There is one temple in the world and that is the body of man. Thou art my brother. In the death of the Phoenix, creation and destruction proceed together. Spiritual bonds unite us all.

A king rules by divine right. Freedom is obedience to the heaven chosen. It cannot be brought to light by the ballot box. Whomever nature has ordered him to obey, man obeys. Hero worship is loyalty to the godlike in man. Religion is the immeasurable ocean we name literature. Göethe is the prophet of this religion. Custom persuades us that by simple repetition the miraculous ceases to be miraculous. The deepest of illusions for destroying wonder are space and time. Time and space are not God, but creations of God. Nature is the time-vesture of God.

All symbols are properly clothes; all forms whereby the spirit manifests itself to sense are clothes. Even the lowest provinces of clothes philosophy have value. The dandy is consecrated to the wearing of clothes for their own sake. He lives to dress. He is devoted to self-worship. The sacred books of the dandiacal self-worship are the fashionable novels. There are contrasting sects in Ireland and Scotland: the drudgical earth worship. They are the impoverished. These two sects divide the unsettled portion of the

British people. Dandyism and drudgism are two bottomless boiling whirlpools. The numbers of both sects increase.

Tailors are not justly treated, but the world will come to recognize the tailor. The hypermetaphorical writing of Teufelsdröckh might become general. Teufelsdröckh is not without a wish to proselytize. Hofrath Heuschrecke tells of the disappearance of Teufelsdröckh, perhaps to Paris to confer with the Saint-Simonians or perhaps to London.

## IV  *Autobiographical Elements*

Parallels between the life of Diogenes Teufelsdröckh and the life of Carlyle are close enough to justify the belief that *Sartor Resartus* is in part autobiographical. H. D. Traill, editor of Carlyle's works, is among those who find evidence of the autobiographical nature of *Sartor Resartus.*

It will be more to the purpose of an introduction to the first volume of this new edition of his works, to confine myself mainly to such details of the author's life as are to be gathered from those passages of *Sartor Resartus,* which can with reasonable certainty be identified as autobiographical. In a sense, no doubt, it might be said that this remarkable work—by some admirers regarded as the greatest, and by none denied to be the most characteristic, of all his writings—is autobiographical from first to last. It is unquestionably a minute and faithful history of Carlyle's intellectual and spiritual experiences, which, of course, is the main thing.[1]

Froude, however, in agreement with Moncure D. Conway,[2] quotes Carlyle to the effect that all of *Sartor Resartus* is symbolical except for the Leith Walk (Rue Saint-Thomas de l'Enfer) incident. Nothing in *Sartor Resartus* (he says) "is fact; symbolized myth all, except that of the incident in the Rue St. Thomas de l'Enfer, which occured quite literally to myself in Leith Walk, during three weeks of total sleeplessness, in which almost my one solace was that of a daily bathe on the sands between Leith and Portebello. Incident was as I went down; coming up I generally felt refreshed for the hour. I remember it well, and could go straight to about the place."[3] Nevertheless, parallels between the life of Carlyle and the life of his hero lead to agreement with C. F. Harrold, who wrote in the introduction of his edition of *Sartor Resartus,* "Though Carlyle later wrote that the whole of the Book was 'symbolical myth all,' he excepted the experience in the Rue De l'Enfer. He might have add-

ed, however, that while much of the external character of
Teufelsdröckh had little in common with himself, the whole story of
the inner struggle and victory was essentially his own."[4] Although
the exact amount of biography that can be found in *Sartor Resartus*
may be disputed, the biographical nature of much of it can hardly
be denied.

## V   The Central Metaphor

Book One of *Sartor Resartus* presents his thesis in the form of a
metaphor of clothes, which is also his central literary device and his
chief means to a reaffirmation of the spiritual nature of the universe. Clothes, he affirms, were once the emblems of the spiritual
worth of those who wore them. In a materialistic time, these clothes
reveal the spiritual poverty of the people who wear them.

All visible things are emblems; what thou seest is not there on its own account; strictly taken, is not there at all: Matter exists only spiritually, and to
represent some Idea and *body* it forth. Hence Clothes, as despicable as we
think them, are so unspeakably significant. Clothes, from the King's mantle
downwards, are emblematic, nor of want only, but of a manifold cunning
Victory over Want. On the other hand, all Emblematic things are properly
Clothes, thought-woven or hand-woven: . . . Nay, if you consider it, what
is Man himself, and his whole terrestrial Life, but an Emblem; a Clothing
or visible Garment for that divine Me of his, cast hither, like a light-
particle, down from Heaven? (*Sartor Resartus*, 57)

His view of the world is an expansion of his clothing metaphor. The
visible universe is the clothing of the spiritual universe. All forms
and events are symbols of a moral order or evidence of an underlying moral decay. The man who can see through the metaphor of the
universe, recognizing its underlying moral order, is the hero appointed by God to lead man from his present decay to order and
life, to retailor his clothing.

## VI   The Development of the Hero

Book Two describes the process whereby the hero Diogenes (born
of God) Teufelsdröckh (devil's dung) is purged of the decaying element in his life to become the son of God. The stages through which
the hero must pass are doubt leading to despair, negation, and disbelief, and *selbst-tödtung* (renunciation of self) leading to clearing

vision and ultimate apprehension and affirmation of the glory of God's universe. The first step in the process is increasing doubt in the divine nature of the universe.

Teufelsdröckh gives us long details of his "fever-paroxysms of Doubt;" his Inquiries concerning Miracles, and the Evidences of religious Faith; and how "in the silent night-watches, still darker in his heart than over sky and earth, he has cast himself before the All-seeing, and with audible prayers cried vehemently for Light, for deliverance from Death and the Grave. Not till after long years, and unspeakable agonies, did the believing heart surrender; sink into spell-bound sleep, under the nightmare, Unbelief; and, in this hag-ridden dream, mistake God's fair living world for a pallid, vacant Hades and extinct Pandemonium. . . ." (92)

The promised pandemonium of religious chaos does arrive after Teufelsdröckh experiences several occupational disappointments and a broken romance.

" 'Farewell, then, Madam!' said he, not without sternness, for his stung pride helped him. She put her hand in his, she looked in his face, tears started to her eyes; in wild audacity he clasped her to his bosom; their lips were joined, their two souls, like two dew-drops, rushed into one,—for the first time, and for the last!" Thus was Teufelsdröckh made immortal by a kiss. And then? Why then—"thick curtains of Night rushed over his soul, as rose the immeasurable Crash of Doom; and through the ruins as of a shivered Universe was he falling, falling, towards the Abyss." (118)

The broken romance, it seems, is the last straw. Hard on the heels of disappointment in love come the sorrows of Teufelsdröckh. These sorrows, Teufelsdröckh instinctively feels, must be met before he can assume the moral and spiritual stature of a man. In the meantime, however, his state grows worse instead of better.

"Doubt had darkened into Unbelief," says he; "shade after goes grimly over your soul, till you have the fixed, starless, Tartarean black." To such readers as have reflected, what can be called reflecting, on man's life, and happily discovered, in contradiction to much Profit-and-Loss Philosophy, speculative and practical, that Soul is *not* synonymous with Stomach; who understand, therefore, in our Friend's words, "that, for man's well-being, Faith is properly the one thing needful; how, with it, Martyrs, otherwise weak, can cheerfully endure the shame and the cross; and without it, Worldlings puke up their sick existence, by suicide, in the midst of luxury:" to such it will be clear that, for a pure moral nature, the loss of his religious Belief was the loss of everything. (129)

Having lost his work, his love, his religion, and even his hope, Teufelsdröckh is at the very depths of distraction. At this point the universe appears to him as an unordered machine, symbolic of his moral chaos. "To me the Universe was all void of Life, of Purpose, of Volition, even of Hostility: it was one huge, dead, immeasurable Steam-engine, rolling on, in its dead indifference, to grind me limb from limb. O, the vast, gloomy, solitary Golgotha, and Mill of Death! Why was the Living banished thither companionless, conscious? Why, if there is no Devil; nay, unless the Devil is your God?" (133).

The despairing Teufelsdröckh must continue his suffering until he is able to turn his thoughts outward. This is accomplished by his realization that suffering must have an end, that, meanwhile, he can meet the worst ordained for him. Carlyle describes the neurotic, ingrown personality slowly turning outward, beginning to right itself:

"Despicable biped! What is the sum-total of the worst that lies before thee? Death? Well, Death; and say the pangs of Tophet too, and all that the Devil and Man may, will or can do against thee! Hast thou not a heart; canst thou not suffer whatsoever it be; and, as a Child of Freedom, though outcast, trample Tophet itself under thy feet, while it consumes thee? Let it come, then; I will meet it and defy it!" And as I so thought, there rushed like a stream of fire over my whole soul; and I shook base Fear away from me forever. I was strong, of unknown strength; a spirit, almost a god. Ever from that time, the temper of my misery was changed: not Fear or whining Sorrow was it, but Indignation and grim fire-eyed Defiance. (134 - 35)

In such manner Teufelsdröckh emerged from his fire baptism. He has proved the strength of his spirit, but he is not yet qualified to be a spiritual leader of man. He has dispersed the chaos from his soul, but he has not yet replaced it with order. "We should rather say that Legion, or the Satanic School, was now pretty well extirpated and cast out, but next to nothing introduced in its room; whereby the heart remains, for the while, in a quiet but no comfortable state" (145).

The last step in his process of moral growth is that of *selbst-tödtung* or *entsagen*. Annihilation of self or renunciation is necessary to spiritual or material leadership. It is the one thing to which every hero must attain and without which no man can qualify as a true leader. It is prerequisite to sincerity, without which heroism is impossible. For Carlyle renunciation is the *sine qua non* of his theory of the hero. In the following passage Teufelsdröckh describes the attainment of *selbst-tödtung* or renunciation:

He says: "The hot Harmattan wind has raged itself out; its howl went silent within me; and the long-deafened soul could now hear. I paused in my wild wanderings; and sat me down to wait, and consider; for it was as if the hour of change drew nigh. I seemed to surrender, to renounce utterly, and say: Fly, then, false shadows of Hope; I will chase you no more, I will believe you no more. And ye too, haggard, spectres of Fear, I care not for you; ye too are all shadows and a lie. Let me rest here: for I am way-weary and life-weary; I will rest here, were it but to die: to die or to live is alike to me; alike insignificant."—And again: "Here, then, as I lay in that CENTRE OF INDIFFERENCE; cast, doubtless by benignant upper Influence, into a healing sleep, the heavy dreams rolled gradually away, and I awoke to a new Heaven and a new Earth. The first preliminary moral Act, Annihilation of Self *(Selbst-tödtung)*, had been happily accomplished; and my mind's eyes were now unscaled, and its hands ungyved." (148 - 49)

Teufelsdröckh has attained renunciation, and with it he has recovered the ability to believe. " 'Fore-shadows, call them rather fore-splendours, of that Truth, and Beginning of Truths, fell mysteriously over my soul. Sweeter than Dayspring to the Shipwrecked in Nova Zembla; ah, like the mother's voice to her little child that strays bewildered, weeping, in unknown tumults; like soft streamings of celestial music to my too-exasperated heart, came that Evangel. The Universe is not dead and demoniacal, a charnel-house with spectres; but godlike, and my Father's!' " (150).

This, in brief, is the pattern of the hero's spiritual development that Carlyle uses with greater or lesser degrees of flexibility in all his biographies. The life of Teufelsdröckh represents Carlyle's model of spiritual development and closely parallels his own experiences to the time of his marriage.

Book Three of *Sartor Resartus* is the message that the authenticated prophet will preach to his century. The world is falling into disorder and chaos. Institutions decay, and man falls ill for want of spiritual nourishment and material guidance.

"Thus, too," continues he, "does an observant eye discern everywhere that saddest spectacle: The Poor perishing, like neglected, foundered Draught-Cattle, of Hunger and Overwork; the Rich, still more wretchedly, of Idleness, Satiety, and Over-growth. The Highest in rank, at length, without honour from . . . tavern-waiters who expect to put it in the bill. Once-sacred Symbols fluttering as empty Pageants, whereof men grudge even the expense; a World becoming dismantled: in one word, the CHURCH fallen speechless, from obesity and apoplexy; the STATE shrunken into a Police Office, straitened to get its pay!" (185)

Order, Carlyle believes, must be reestablished among men. A scripture for the nineteenth century must be written, and a master for the masterless must be found. "For the present, it is contemplated that when man's whole Spiritual Interests are once *divested*, these unnumerable stript-off Garments shall mostly be burnt; but the sounder Rags among them be quilted together into one huge Irish watch-coat for the defence of the Body only!—This, we think, is but Job's-news to the humane reader" (187). Whatever changes, Carlyle concludes, one thing, the divine right of a king to rule, remains unalterable.

"The only Title wherein I, with confidence, trace eternity, is that of King. König (King), anciently Könning, means Ken-ning (Cunning), or which is the same thing, Can-ning. Ever must the Sovereign of Mankind be fitly entitled King."

"Well, also," says he elsewhere, "was it written by Theologians: a King rules by divine right. He carries in him an authority from God, or man will never give it him. Can I choose my own King? I can choose my own King Popinjay, and play what farce or tragedy I may with him: but he who is to be my Ruler, whose will is to be higher than my will, was chosen for me in Heaven. Neither except in such Obedience to the Heaven-chosen is Freedom so much as conceivable." (198)

Besides a true king, all that is needed for order is a true religion. This religion is to be supplied by literature. " 'But there is no Religion?' reiterates the Professor. 'Fool! I tell thee, there is. Hast thou well considered all that lies in this immeasurable froth-ocean we name LITERATURE? Fragments of a genuine Church-*Homiletic* lie scattered there, which Time will assort: nay fractions even of a *Liturgy* could I point out.' " (201 - 202). The God-appointed ruler, Carlyle believes, is certified by suffering, annihilation of self, and efforts in the name of order, which is ever divine will.

*Sartor Resartus* is a literary expression of the experiences that turned Carlyle to the writing of biographies of heroes and leaders. The message of Teufelsdröckh's life is the message Carlyle consistently advocated: abandon self; merge with divine order.

## VII  *Archtypal Elements*

The life of Teufelsdröckh contains incidents that resemble experiences of other heroes. The reader catches glimpses of Göethe's Werther, whose despair over lost love leads him to suicide, of Byron's Manfred, who proclaims man's existential loneliness, or of Job, whose suffering probes the pith of mortal paradox. Carlyle was familiar with works that describe the hero exiled from society and from self, but his indebtedness to them is slight. The life of Teufelsdröckh is archtypal rather than derivative. Born of unknown lineage and discovered under mysterious circumstances by foster parents, Teufelsdröckh grows to manhood in bucolic surroundings, is rejected by the woman he loves, loses faith in all values, and becomes an exile from self and from society.

When he named his hero Diogenes (born of God) Teufelsdröckh (devil's dung), Carlyle saw him partaking of equal portions of good and evil. His appearance at the home of the Futterals on an evening during the autumnal equinox is a reinforcement of the balance of the elements contained in his nature. As Teufelsdröckh, he must suffer from doubt and isolation. As Diogenes, he must affirm order and meaning. Diogenes Teufelsdröckh is everyman, and every man embraces "The Everlasting No," "The Center of Indifference," and "The Everlasting Yea." Only the hero can sort out and reject the negative elements of life, overcome indifference, and move steadily to affirmation.

*Sartor Resartus* states the main principles that Carlyle follows in all his writing. As time passes, he speaks out with greater anger against negation or indifference. The expression of his position becomes extreme; reiterations become tiresome; heroes become more practical; nevertheless, the basic principles of *Sartor Resartus* are never abandoned.

### CHAPTER 6

# Carlyle's Style

I delight in the contents; the form, which my defective apprehension for a joke makes me not appreciate, I leave to your merry discretion," wrote Emerson from Boston, May 14, 1834, upon reading Carlyle's *Sartor Resartus,* which was then appearing in *Fraser's Magazine.*[1] His complaint of Carlyle's "defying diction" and "spend-thrift style" became standard comment in the years that followed its publication, and even today readers of the book may be confounded by the way in which it is written. In *Sartor Resartus,* Carlyle's passionate tone, unconventional syntax, and unusual diction transcend traditional style by so much that the reader responds to them far more readily than to how they are used. Yet the style of *Sartor Resartus* is not a style resulting entirely from Carlyle's personality, nor is it borrowed from contemporaries or predecessors, English or foreign. It is, rather, the result of Carlyle's effort to discover a manner in which he might speak to the readers of his day.

Pleased with Emerson's friendly letter, Carlyle responded to his friend's query concerning style with comments clear, perhaps, only to those who were familiar with his concerns as a writer.

With regard to style and so forth, . . . my view is that now at last we have lived to see all manner of Poetics and Rhetorics and Sermonics, and one may say generally all manner of *Pulpits* for addressing mankind from, as good as broken and abolished: . . . and so one leaves the pasteboard coulisses, and three unities, and Blair's Lectures, quite behind; and feels only that there is *nothing sacred,* then, but the *Speech of Man* to believing Men! . . . Meanwhile, I know no method of much consequence, except that of *believing,* of being *sincere:* from Homer and the Bible down to the poorest Burns's Song, I find no other Art that promises to be perennial. (*Correspondence, Emerson,* I, 22 - 24)

Perhaps Emerson found Carlyle's explanation unrevealing. At any rate, by 1835, he apparently accepted the view expressed by A. H.

Everett in the *North American Review* that Carlyle's style "may be a mere result of a great familiarity with German literature";[2] for writing to Carlyle in October of the popularity of *Sartor Resartus*, he warns, "Don't think I speak of myself, for I cherish carefully a salutary horror at the German style and hold off my admiration as long as ever I can" *(Correspondence, Emerson,* I, 84). From this time hence, Carlyle's style became a concern for readers and reviewers. In writing *Sartor Resartus,* Carlyle created a style so far removed from convention that it startled readers into angry denunciation of it. Furthermore, in spite of vigorous remonstrance, Carlyle persisted in his defection from contemporary standards.

## I  *The Influence of German Writers*

In a sense Everett's and Emerson's views are well founded. Carlyle's years of German study were apprentice years in an extraordinary way and to an extraordinary degree. His style, though not an imitation or importation, is largely the result of his years of German study. The ideas he formulated during that time are closely related to German thought on the one hand and to the way in which he wrote on the other *(Two Notebooks,* 150 - 151). Many such ideas are expressed in his notebooks, letters, and publications of the 1820's; and the source of most of them can be found in Fichte, Schiller, Richter, Göethe, Novalis, Schelling, or Kant.[3] Yet the form that they take and the use to which they are put are increasingly subjected to his own Calvinistic beliefs. In the German writers, he found justification for subordinating literature to a spiritual order. "Poetic beauty," he writes, ". . . dwells and is born in the inmost Spirit of Man, united to all love of Virtue, to all true belief in God; or rather, it is one with this love and this belief, another phase of the same highest principle in the mysterious infinitude of the human Soul" *(Essays,* I, 55 - 56). German letters gave him all the encouragement he needed to reject the theories of literature from Hume to Alison, including association, "reminiscences of mere sensations," natural love, imitation, "excitement by contrast," or "seeing difficulties overcome."

By April 1832, what he had found congenial in German aesthetics takes the form most suitable to his mind and purpose. He records in his notebook, "The grand Pulpit is now the Press; the true Church (as I have said twenty times of late) is the Guild of Authors" *(Two Notebooks,* 263). In a later entry he writes, "Every man that writes is writing a new Bible; or a new Apocrypha; to last for a week, or for a thousand years: he that convinces a man and sets him working is the doer of a *miracle*" *(Two Notebooks,* 264). Carlyle adapted what he found in German letters to the climate of his mind. The transcendental aesthetic, as Carlyle understood it, seemed to free the writer from all strictly intellectual constraints. By accepting ideas authorized by German writers, Carlyle effected a synthesis of the good and the beautiful and justified any departure he might wish to make from traditional English usage.

## II   *German Influence on Carlyle's Point of View*

In addition to justifying his subjectivism, German thought supported Carlyle's tendency to see things through metaphor. He is indebted to Fichte and Göethe for the concept that enabled him to free his writings from the restraints of conventional rhetoric (Blair's lectures) as well as to rationalize his religious position. Style became the clothing of belief. Old forms were justified as long as they carried out their functions convincingly. If they lost their effectiveness, became conventions only, they must be abandoned in favor of the new. Though truth remained ever the same, it could not be represented in the same manner for every generation.

According to Fichte there is a "Divine Idea" pervading the visable Universe; which visable Universe is indeed but its symbol and sensible manifestation, having in itself no meaning, or even true existence independent of it. To the mass of men this Divine Idea of the world lies hidden: . . . Literary men are the appointed interpreters of this Divine Idea; a perpetual priesthood, we might say, standing forth, generation after generation, as the dispensers and living types of God's everlasting wisdom, . . . in such particular form as their times require it in. For each age by the law of its nature, is different from every other age, and demands a different representation of the Divine Idea, the essence of which is the same in all; . . . *(Essays,* I, 58)

Carlyle's belief that each age requires its own statement of the divine idea is consistent with his statement to Emerson that "we have lived to see all manner of Pulpits for addressing mankind from, as good as broken and abolished." His acceptance of the symbolic nature of the universe lies at the center of his literary method.

In August of 1830, he writes in his notebook, "All Language but that concerning *sensual* objects is or has been figurative. Prodigious influence of metaphors! Never saw into it till lately. A truly useful work would be a good *Essay on Metaphors*. Some day I will write one!" *(Two Notebooks,* 141 - 42). For Carlyle the German concept became technique; however, he did not understand the metaphor as a figure of speech only. It was both a window through which one might see into the nature of the universe and the poet's way of expressing spiritual truth. Carlyle need not have gone to German thought for this idea, but he did. The Germans share with Calvinism, Swift, Sir Thomas Brown, and the Bible the responsibility for Carlyle's metaphorical vision; for they all seem to have contributed to its particular development in Carlyle's writing. Carlyle's treatment of the physical world as the metaphor of spiritual reality is the basis of his style, and his writings are filled with unexpected applications of it. Action, physical appearance, and language itself are expressions of its condition. Thus, German literature not only supported Carlyle's faith in God and his dissatisfaction with the church of his day but also provided him with a point of view that encouraged the development of an apocalyptic style. It furnished a way to regain and maintain his deepest convictions while allowing him to attack the church and the religious thought of his time. It gave him the status of priest and prophet while it provided him with a justification for his departure from conventions. Such thinking preceded the writing of *Sartor Resartus,* begun shortly after September 28, 1830.

### III    *The Influence of Kant*

Kantean concepts of time and space also influenced Carlyle's style. In writing of Novalis in 1829, Carlyle acknowledged a timeless and spaceless universe. "But further, and what is still stranger than such Idealism, according to these Kantean systems, the organs of the Mind too, what is called the Understanding, are of no less arbitrary, and, as it were accidental character than those of the Body. Time and Space themselves are not external but internal entities: they have no outward existence, there is no Time and no Space *out* of the mind; they are mere *forms* of man's spiritual being, *laws* under which his thinking nature is constituted to act" *(Essays,* II, 25 - 26). Like others, this idea is recorded in his notebook adapted to his own purpose. "But on the whole our conception of Immortality (as Dreck too has it) depends on that of *Time;* . . . Believe that there properly *is* no Space and no Time, how many contradictions become reconciled!" *(Two Notebooks,*

221 - 22) If time and space are ideas only, history itself becomes the record of divine will. Man's physical state becomes an expression of his ability to relate himself to timelessness and spacelessness. The more faithless the people, the more securely are they held by concepts of time and space.

Finally, German thought provided Carlyle with a critical view that made the barbs of the reviewers harmless, if still painful. In his essay "Göethe" (1828), Carlyle points out that a literary fault is simply something that displeases the reader or contradicts his views. If, however, the author truly embodies divine realities in his writing, what the reader sees as faults may be the result of his own spiritual inadequacy. Carlyle's view leads him safely out of the hands of the critics. He concedes that a writer may have only the pleasure of the reader in mind. In such case, the reader may indeed have a basis for complaint. But the writer who embodies divine truth in his work is answerable only to God (*Essays*, I, 253 - 54). "Every man that writes is writing a new Bible; or a new Apocrypha."

The critical views Carlyle expressed in his letter to Emerson in 1834 are expressed with considerably more clarity a year later when he responded to an interested appraisal of *Sartor Resartus* by John Sterling, who also questioned the style of the book. Answering Sterling's charges of the "lawless oddity" of his "rhapsodico-reflective" method June 4, 1835, Carlyle defends his style with the same argument he had used before.

Know thy thought, *believe* it; front Heaven and Earth with it,—in whatsoever *words* Nature and Art have made readiest for thee! . . . I see nothing for it but that you must use words not found there, must *make* words,—with moderation and discretion, of course. That I have not always done it *so*, proves only that I was not strong enough; an accusation to which I for one will never plead not guilty. . . . But finally, do you reckon this really a time for Purism of Style; or that Style (mere dictionary Style) has much to do with the worth or unworth of a Book? I do not: with whole ragged battalions of Scott's-Novel Scotch, with Irish, German, French, and even Newspaper Cockney (when "Literature" is little other than a Newspaper) storming in on us, and the whole structure of our Johnsonian English breaking up from its foundations,—revolution *there* as visible as anywhere else![4]

As before, Carlyle records his belief in a journal. "The poor people seem to think a style can be put off or put on, not like a skin but like a coat. Is not a skin verily a product and close kinsfellow of all that lies under it, exact type of the nature of the beast, not to be plucked off without flaying and death? The Public is an old woman. Let her maunder and mumble."[5] Carlyle was fully aware of his style and of its purpose.

## IV  *Carlyle's Style and Belief*

Carlyle's style was a relatively slow synthesis of Calvinistic dogma and German idealism, achieved painfully, only after bitter self-evaluation. *Sartor Resartus* is at once the record and the monument of his struggle to reach a synthesis satisfactory to him. The cost of his achievement can be measured by the increasing acerbity of his personality and the alternating periods of hopelessness and confidence that characterize his biography. The entire process, accompanied by sympathetic physiological responses, is marked by his constant awareness of his position.

Writing in his notebook in November 1823, Carlyle describes his condition in language similar to what would become his mature expression. "My time! My time! My peace and activity! My hopes and purposes! Where are they? I could read the curse of Ernulphus, or something twenty times as fierce, upon myself and all things earthly. What *will* become of me? Happiness! Tophet must be happier than this: or they—But *basta!* It is no use talking. Let me get on with Schiller; then with Göethe" (*Two Notebooks*, 51). His correspondence to his friends and family bears the same lament, often associating his physical with his psychological state; but his sharpest complaints are expressed when he undertook original composition. His letters to Jane Welsh contain frequent comments on his difficulty in writing. In February 1823, he writes to her in real despair.

— Oh! I could beat my brains out when I think what a miserable, pithless ninny I am! Would it were in my power either to write like a man or honestly to give up the attempt for ever. Chained to the earth by native gravitation and a thousand wretched fetters, I am miserable unless I be soaring in the empyrean; and thus between the lofty will and the powerless deed, I have no peace, no peace. Sometimes I could almost run distracted; my wearied soul seems as if it were hunted round within its narrow enclosure by a whole legion of the dogs of Tartarus, which sleep not, night or day. (*Early Letters*, 266)

The similarity between Carlyle's complaints of ill health and troubles with writing suggest a closer relationship to Job than simply that of his favorite biblical reading (109). Indeed, the entire body of his work bears the print of a painful personal concern that relates his fully developed style to the complaints of ill health in his letters. The quality of Carlyle's response to what he believed he must do adds a personal dimension to his style.

Nevertheless, Carlyle's chief problem was not with what he wanted to write. It was with how he could believe what he wanted to write and how he could write it so that it would be believed by others. His Edinburgh education had taught him a logic that destroyed the foundations of his boyhood religion, yet he persisted in a religious belief. German thought and criticism taught him, he believed, how to meet the arguments of mechanistic thought. During most of the 1820s, however, his struggle was the effort to justify the demonstrable facts of science and history with what he believed. After he had settled that problem, the struggle to present his vision convincingly to others continued. The conclusion of the first phase of his struggle is recorded in his notebook for March 1830. He writes, "I think I have got rid of Materialism: Matter no longer seems to me so ancient, so unsubduable, so *certain* and palpable as Mind. *I* am Mind: whether matter or not I know not—can care not.—Mighty glimpses into the spiritual Universe I have sometimes had (about the true nature of Religion, the possibility, after all, of 'supernatural' (really natural) influences &c. &c.): would they could but stay with me, and ripen into a perfect view!" (*Two Notebooks*, 151). By autumn of that year, his efforts bore results. His style and his religious convictions coalesced.

On October 19, 1830, he wrote to his brother John of a new work. His letter is confident and self-assured. "What I am writing at is the strangest of all things: begun as an Article for *Fraser;* then found to be too long (except it were divided into two); now sometimes looking as if it would swell into a Book. A very singular piece, I assure you! It glances from Heaven to Earth and back again in a strange satirical frenzy, whether *fine* or not remains to be seen."[6] To his notebook he confided more of his purpose: his desire to speak for God and of God to man. "Canst *thou* in any measure spread abroad Reverence over the hearts of men? That were a far higher task than *any* other. Is it to be done by Art; or are men's minds as yet shut to Art, and open only at best to oratory; not fit for a *Meister*, but only for a better and better *Teufelsdreck; Denk' und schweig!*" (*Two Notebooks*, 203 - 204). Carlyle's literary maturity dates from the writing of *Sartor Resartus*. Thereafter his style varied just enough to suit the occasion of his writing.

## V    *The Influence of Richter*

Other theories of Carlyle's style have frequently been expressed. Henry David Thoreau, writing of Carlyle in 1847, notes that "in his graphic description of Richter's style, Carlyle describes his own pretty nearly; and no doubt he first got his own tongue loosened at that fountain, and was inspired by it to equal freedom and originality."[7] Froude asserts that Carlyle's style was "learnt in the Annandale farmhouse,"[8] and reports that Carlyle himself said his style was much more influenced by the old puritans and Elizabethans than by Richter, but most of all by his boyhood environment.[9] Others have suggested the influence of the Bible, of pulpit orators, and of Swift. All contentions contain some truth.[10] But the suggestion that Carlyle's style is an English echo of Jean Paul Richter is frequently repeated.

Still, there is little doubt that Richter influenced Carlyle, who translated his work in *German Romance* and wrote two critical essays and one critical notice concerning him. As Thoreau pointed out, Carlyle writes of Richter's style in a way that describes his own writing; however, neither Carlyle's translations of Richter nor an observation of Richter's prose suggests a parallel nearly so close as Carlyle's description leads one to suspect. Still, a comparison of Carlyle's style with his translation of Richter and with selections from Richter's writing leads this writer to the conclusion that a relationship between the two writers does exist. Carlyle uses a limited number of Richter's words and expressions; he employs an unconventional syntax, as does Richter; and he attempts the wry humor of the German writer. That these or other points of similarity are evident does not, however, account for Carlyle's style. When the complex and personal nature of Carlyle's style is recognized, Richter's part must be reduced to a minor role.

Carlyle is beyond the ordinary, a writer whose style must be considered related to his aim in writing. Throughout his career, he valued literature chiefly for its moral function. When it is didactive or corrective, Carlyle accepted it. When it is a hymn of praise for the divine, he called it poetry. But whenever it served purposes of aesthetic pleasure only, he found it oppressive. He was not a literary man in the present sense of the word. Important literary movements of his age failed to impress him except for their religious implications. For Carlyle, as for his parents and the social group of his childhood, all activities were secondary to the workings of a Calvinistic universe. The riddle of Carlyle's style is not solved by tracing influences or by drawing parallels. It is directly related to his central purpose: to speak out concerning the nature of God and the nature of God's universe. His purpose and his style developed between the years 1820 and 1832, following an unusually painful rejection of orthodox Calvinistic theology. *Sartor Resartus* is both the record of this process and the point at which his purpose and his style converge.

## VI   *Purpose and Style*

Carlyle's vision was that the spiritual nature of the universe is written out in negative or positive fashion in the lives and actions of men of every age. Some ages, Carlyle believed, are prosaic. These are ages of doubt and theological controversy. Other ages are poetic, thus ages of the celebration of God. All matter speaks out its response to God in one way or another. Carlyle's purpose in writing was to point out this truth to his age in a way understandable to all. He consistently fashions his language to reveal his underlying purpose. He selected the fact, the word, the phrase for what it revealed about the deeper nature of his subject.

The harmony of style with purpose is characteristic of Carlyle's prose. Here he can be seen as an artist; for, in spite of the impression of chaos and eccentricity, his prose follows rigorous artistic procedures. The following paragraph from *Sartor Resartus* illustrates how Carlyle's prose reveals his intentions.

"Into this umbrageous Man's-nest, one meek yellow evening or dusk, when the Sun hidden indeed from terrestrial Entepfuhl, did nevertheless journey visable and radiant along the celestial Balance *(Libra)*, it was that a Stranger of reverend aspect entered; and, with grave salutation, stood before the two rather astonished housemates. He was close-muffled in a wide mantle; which without farther parley unfolding, he deposited therefrom what seemed some Basket, overhung with green Persian silk; saying only: *Ihr lieben Leute, hier bringe ein unschatzbares Verleihen; nehmt es in aller Acht, sorgfaltigst benutzt es: mit hohem Lohn, oder wohl mit schweren Zinsen, wird's einst zuruckgefordert.* 'Good Christian people, here lies for you an invaluable Loan; take all heed thereof, in all carefulness employ it: with high recompense, or else with heavy penalty, will it one day be required back.' Uttering which singular words, in a clear, bell like, forever memorable tone, the Stranger gracefully withdrew; and before Andreas or his wife, gazing in expectant wonder, had time to fashion either question or answer, was clean gone. Neither out of doors could aught of him be seen or heard; he had vanished in the thickets, in the dusk; the Orchard-gate stood quietly closed: the Stranger was gone once and always. So sudden had the whole transaction been, in the autumn stillness and twilight, so gentle, noiseless, that the Futterals could have fancied it all a trick of Imagination, or some visit from an authentic Spirit. Only that the green-silk Basket, such as neither Imagination nor authentic Spirits are wont to carry, still stood visable and tangible on their little parlour-table. Toward this the astonished couple, now with lit candle, hastily turned their attention. Lifting the green veil, to see what invaluable it hid, they descried there, amid down and rich white wrappages, no Pitt Diamond or Hapsburg Regalia, but, in the softest sleep, a little red-coloured Infant! Beside it, lay a roll of gold Friedrichs, the exact amount of which was never publicly known; also a *Taufschein* (baptismal certificate), wherein unfortunately nothing but the Name was decipherable; other document or indication none whatever. (66 - 67)

Characteristic of the way in which Carlyle's language supports his central purpose, dramatic tension brings expansion, inversion, connotation, and allusion into unity.

The first sentence, stated conventionally, reads, A stranger stepped into a house and stood before the housemates one evening. By inversion, amplification, and the introduction of dramatic tensions, Carlyle makes of it something more than a declarative topic sentence. Selecting his words with an eye to their connotations, he begins, "Into this umbrageous Man's-nest, . . ." *Man's-nest*, suggesting *mare's nest*, a place or situation of great disorder, restricts the associations conveyed by the common noun *home* to a place of shelter until maturity is reached. *Into*, appearing at the beginning of the sentence, places emphasis upon the intrusion of the dramatic. Thus, at the outset of his paragraph, Carlyle depicts a dramatic situation that has extensional significance. The tone of the passage is heightened by the use of noun and adjective from classes of English words not usually coupled: the Latin borrowing and the vernacular. Adding more detail, he expands his phrase by adding "one meek yellow evening or dusk" to specify the time and to introduce his imagery of light and dark. Within the house all is shadow; without lies ambiguous light and dark that he calls "meek yellow" rather than "yellow" to subdue the brilliance of the color. The introduction of an amplifying adverbial clause, "when the sun, hidden indeed from terrestial Entepfuhl, did nevertheless journey visible and radiant along the celestial Balance *(Libra),"* emphasizes the time of day and indicates the specific day of the year by reference to the zodiac. Once again dramatic tension is established, this time suggesting a cosmic balance in the total situation. The sun hidden, though visibly radiant, behind the vegetation of Entepfuhl dramatically opposes the son radiantly red beneath the green silk of the basket. Teufelsdröckh's appearance coincides with the time of day when light and dark are in balance with the time of year, the autumnal equinox, when day and night are equal, but when the larger context, the hemisphere, enters a period of growing darkness.

What we learn of Diogenes Teufelsdröckh's life and personality is consonant with his origin. The baptismal certificate establishes no parentage. The origin of Carlyle's hero is hidden from view, but the specific reference to the time and to light and dark suggests that his appearance has cosmic importance for light or dark, for good or for evil. Although additional information can be drawn from this passage, enough has been pointed out to illustrate the purposive nature of Carlyle's style of writing.

## VII  *Dramatic Elements*

The dramatic tension observable in Carlyle's use of language appears in the structure and diction of every book he wrote. In his use of imagery, tension is usually found between light and dark colors. In abstractions, tension is found between order and chaos, health and illness, work and idleness. His language evokes the larger conflict at the heart of all his writing: the conflict between good and evil.

Dramatic tension serves Carlyle in many ways. It permits him the greatest latitude in his attacks on what he sees as evil: it can be applied to any biography, history, philosophy, or social institution; it is so timeless and placeless in human experience that it is an easily managed universal; it serves as a method of exposition and as a demonstration of divine will; it allows Carlyle to speak in either of its two voices as an impartial observer and permits him to introduce real or straw figures as opponents or heroes; finally, it encourages him to make an emotionally significant interpretation of what he views. Often, as in the passage describing the genesis of Teufelsdröckh, it enables Carlyle to assign cosmic importance to comparatively insignificant or completely contradictory details.

The simplicity of dramatic tension as a technical device is disproportionate to its effectiveness. Heroes are described in terms of order, light, fire, noble beasts, degrees of perception, or types of vision. Villains become chaos, darkness, cold, ignoble creatures, or beings who lack perception or have distorted vision. Observers are neutral, light-seeking, or dark-seeking. Carlyle's heroes may even contend with unembodied evil, the chaotic spirit of the age. Carlyle's dramatic tensions are expressed in seemingly endless variations. On the other hand, some are used so often that Carlyle can evoke them with a single word or phrase, often little more than an epithet. Others are modified with an eye for the more pungent expression. For the practiced reader of Carlyle's prose, the dramatic tensions take on increasingly richer associations.

The hero's role in the conflict between good and evil does not always end favorably for him. At times he falls in the midst of battle. His fall, however, is generally understood to be the result of some spiritual weakness that, as in the case of John Sterling, whose death resulted from disease, is "the expression, under physical conditions, of the too vehement life which, under the moral, the intellectual and other aspects, incessantly struggled within him."[11] His villains, on the other hand, are nearly always the embodiment of whatever is false or chaotic. Cagliostro, for example, is not described historically. He is presented through a wealth of epithets and references that describe his moral worth but in no way analyze his historical importance.

> On such desirable second-best, perhaps the chief of all such, we have here found in the Count Alessandro di Cagliostro, Pupil of the Sage Althotas, Foster-child of the Scherif of Mecca, probable Son of the last King of Trebisond; named also Acharat, and Unfortunate Child of Nature; by profession healer of diseases, abolisher of wrinkles, friend of the poor and impotent, grand-master of the Egyptian Mason-lodge of High Science, Spirit-summoner, Gold-cook, Grand Cophta, Prophet, Priest, and thaumaturgic moralist and swindler; really a Liar of the first magnitude, thorough-paced in all provinces of lying, what one may call the King of Liars. (*Essays*, III, 254 - 55)

The painting of heroism or villainy is an art to which Carlyle applies all the skill at his command.

### VIII   *Metaphor and Style*

As an element characterizing Carlyle's style, the metaphor is as important as dramatic tension. Carlyle used all types of metaphors in his prose, but his central metaphor, the Fichtean notion that the phenomenon is the embodiment of the noumenon, is almost always at work. Frederick the Great's asure grey eyes and "snuffy nose . . . like an old snuffy lion on the watch," Mirabeau's "giant oaken strength," John Sterling's rapidity, as well as Cagliostro's falsehood are the visable expression of spiritual characteristics. Carlyle's desire to have possession of visible facts led him into minute examination of portraits, as in the case of John Knox and Cromwell; and some of his most vivid attacks fall upon historians and biographers who fail to provide him with the concrete details that he requires to reach his perception of the spiritual nature of the man or time. In his review of Naigeon's life of Diderot (1821), for example, he complains, "Foolish Naigeon! We wanted to see and know how it stood with the bodily man, the clothed, boarded, bedded, working and war-faring Denis Diderot, in that Paris of his; how he looked and lived, what he did, what he said: had the foolish Biographer so much as told us what colour his stockings were!" (*Essays*, III, 183).

Critical of writers who gave hin insufficient detail upon which to base his metaphor, Carlyle also rejected those who presented him with facts only. They became the "Dryasdusts" familiar to his readers. His practice of drawing moral judgment of a man by the in-terpretation of concrete details nearly always results in vivid reading. The method is not restricted, however, to the analysis of human character; it is also employed in his reading of historical periods. In "Signs of The Times" (1829), Carlyle characterizes his own age as a mechanical one, ". . . not an Heroical, Devotional, Philosophical, or Moral Age, but, above all others, the Mechanical Age. It is the Age of Machinery, in every outward and inward sense of that word . . ." (II, 59); and concludes that " 'the deep meaning of the Laws of Mechanism lies heavy on us'; and in the closet, in the marketplace, in the temple, by the social hearth, encumbers the whole movements of our mind, and over our noblest faculties is spreading a nightmare sleep" (79 - 80).

Finally, Carlyle's metaphor led him to the conclusion that time and space are essentially meaningless. The life of every man, every society, and every age was basically the same, a dramatic struggle between order and chaos. The most obvious result of his metaphorical treatment of time and space is his assumption that things do not change, that actions anywhere in every age are related to the spiritual force he recognized in his own. He measured men of the past by the same criteria he used to judge men of his own day and thus brought to his histories all the vividness of personal acquaintance. He understood Abbot Samson's twelfth century problems in the same way as he understood Governor Eyre's in the nineteenth century. The problems of Luther were essentially those of Irving; those of Shakespeare were those of Coleridge. "For at bottom the Great Man," wrote Carlyle, "as he comes from the hand of Nature, is ever the same kind of thing: I hope to make it appear that these are all originally of one stuff; that only by the world's reception of them, and the shapes they assume, are they so immeasurably diverse:"[12] By disregarding the special circumstances of time and space and by relating all characteristics of society to a spiritual absolute, Carlyle made good his promise. All that is needed for any age is the man or men who can read the open and unchanging mystery of God's universe and apply that eternal power to his own age. Never does Carlyle speak so clearly to this point as in the *Latter-Day Pamphlets* (1850). "The Present Time," a vigorous summary of his position, insists that the need for any country at any time or place is the working recognition of divine order.

Alas, on this side of the Atlantic and on that, Democracy, we apprehend, is forever impossible! So much, with certainty of loud astonished contradiction from all manner of men at present, but with sure appeal to the Law of Nature and the ever-abiding Fact, may be suggested and asserted once more. The Universe itself is a Monarchy and Hierarchy; large liberty of "voting" there, all manner of choice, utmost free-will, but with conditions inexorable and immeasurable annexed to every exercise of the same. A most free commonwealth of "voters"; but with Eternal Justice to preside over it, Eternal Justice enforced by Almighty Power! This is the model of "constitutions"; this: nor in any Nation where there has not yet (in some supportable and withal some constantly-increasing degree) been confided to the *Noblest*, with his select series of *Nobler*, the divine everlasting duty of directing and controlling the Ignoble, has the "Kingdom of God," which we all pray for, "come," nor can "His will" even *tend* to be "done on Earth as it is in Heaven" till then. My Christian friends, and indeed my Sham-Christian and Anti-Christian, and all manner of men, are invited to reflect on this. They will find it to be the truth of the case. The Noble in the high place, the Ignoble in the low; that is, in all times and in all countries, the Almighty Maker's Law. (*LDP*, 21 - 22)

Carlyle's difficulty for critics today is closely related to modern concepts of the divine, which do not tolerate Carlyle's absolute God.

Carlyle's treatment of time and space as departures from divine reality reduces government to its simplest terms. Good government is government patterned on God's eternal law; good governors are divinely ordained for the purpose of enforcing God's will. History is the record of man's successes and failures to live by the divine law. "Is not Man's History and Men's History, a perpetual Evangel?" asks Teufelsdröckh *(Sartor Resartus,* 202). Granted the meaninglessness of time and space, Carlyle can subject all humanistic studies to his metaphor that sees matter as the clothing of spirit. "Pierce through the Time-element, glance into the Eternal," he writes. "Believe what thou findest written in all the sanctuaries of Man's Soul, even as all Thinkers, in all ages, have devoutly read it there: that Time and Space are not God, but creations of God; that with God as it is a universal HERE, so is it an everlasting Now" (208).

## IX  *Conclusion*

Carlyle's style is the expression of an extraordinary synthesis of ideas and modes of thinking drawn from his home environment, his reading of German writers, and his personal experience. Measured against his purpose, rather than against some external standard, as he, himself, urges in his criticism of other writers, Carlyle's style proves to be a highly effective means for the expression of his message.

CHAPTER 7

# The Biographies:
# Schiller, Cromwell, and Sterling

CARLYLE was not satisfied writing articles for the reviews, even though his work received considerable attention. Because his inspiration had been derived from the German writers, he naturally turned to them as subjects for his early work; but, when it became obvious to him that British readers would never develop any great admiration for German transcendentalism, Carlyle stated his opinions in his own name. His difficulties were many. The need of an immediate and regular income turned him to the writing of books. That his opinions stoutly challenged every basic trend of the time did not make his road smoother. In an age of change, Carlyle preached the unchanging. To an age that heralded *laissez faire* in economy and equality in government, Carlyle asserted the benefits of political oligarchy. With few exceptions, the aim of his writing is moral instruction, and the medium through which he presents his lessons is biography that follows a stated method amplified by practice and controlled by his moral purpose.

Carlyle's biographies follow the pattern that was established in the biographical essays. He began his career as a biographer with the publication of *The Life of Schiller* (1825) and concluded it with the publication of *The History of Frederick the Great* (1858 - 1865). The change in subject from the poet to the ruler recalls the same change in the essays. The intermediate state, represented in the essays by imperfect heroes such as Burns and Voltaire, is not represented by a full length biography; but *The Life of John Sterling* (1851), which presents the life of a subject ordinarily not important enough to merit such a study, bridges the gap. The hero on the level of action is presented in two full length studies: *Oliver Cromwell's Letters and Speeches* (1845) and *Frederick the Great*. The latter is a study of an imperfect political hero who is Carlyle's

73

final offer to an age that had shot the Niagara of disbelief and was, in his opinion, well on its way to the whirlpool of social and moral chaos.

Carlyle's four long biographies confirm much of what has been found to be true of the biographical essays; but because they also contribute additions to his theory of the hero and to the development of his thought, they must be considered. That his biographies were motivated by religious conviction becomes more evident as his writing and his ideas mature. Even in his earliest biography, however, his sympathy for his subject proclaims the subjective involvement and interpretative tendency that become more pronounced as time passes. As these elements in his writing take shape, Carlyle's importance as a thinker and as a literary man is defined.

## I   The Life of Schiller

When Carlyle finished *The Life of Schiller* in 1824, he was yet in his literary apprenticeship.[1] He had, indeed, written the biographical entries for the *Edinburgh Encyclopaedia* and translated Legendre's *Elements of Geometry and Trigonometry* and Göethe's *Wilhelm Meister's Apprenticeship*, but *The Life of Schiller* was his first original work. The book has many of the characteristics of a first volume: it is not tightly organized; some confusion results when Carlyle turns his attention from the poet's life to his poetry; interest aroused in the details of Schiller's life is sometimes not satisfied; quotations from the poetic dramas are longer than necessary; and the style of writing is not indicative of what was later to come from the same hand. Still, the basic characteristics of *The Life of Schiller* are those that the reader will find strengthened and clarified in his later works.

A glance into the early chapters of the biography is sufficient to reveal Carlyle's sympathy for German transcendentalism and for those who practice it. A somewhat more careful inspection reveals, perhaps, that Carlyle's dependency on interpretation of factual material may have begun as the result of the paucity of biographical data available to him. He had little aid from libraries and none at all from anyone who had known the poet personally. The absence of details of the poet's early life leads Carlyle to draw as many inferences as possible from the writings of the poet, and his ability to achieve credibility in so doing drew a somewhat surprised, though congratulatory, response from Göethe, who wrote to him, "The accurate insight into the character and distinguished merit of this man, which you have thus acquired is really admirable, and so clear and just as was hardly to have been expected from a foreigner."[2] Göethe's response to Carlyle's *Schiller* was mixed with gratitude; for in 1827, Carlyle was among the few writers in English who found much to admire in German poets or their poetry.

Schiller, Göethe, and other German poets are the direct source of Carlyle's early admiration of the *Vates*-poet, who was to remain Carlyle's ideal hero, even though he was abandoned later for heroes of a more practical nature. Carlyle finds Schiller to have the "half-poetical, half philosophical imagination" that enables the poet to probe the "abysses of thought and feeling" that were essential functions of his hero. Schiller's ability to grasp depths of thought and feeling, Carlyle believed, was the result of "sceptical doubts on the most important of all subjects" (*Schiller*, 49) that lead him first to soul crisis and later to renunciation of self. "His great, almost his single aim," Carlyle writes, "was to unfold his spiritual faculties, to study and contemplate and improve their intellectual creations . . . At all times he was far above the meanness of self-interest, particularly in its meanest shape, a love of money" (196). The experiences necessary for the development of the hero are clearly apparent in the biography of Schiller.

Additional characteristics later incorporated into his system of biography are also present in *Schiller*. The poet and his biographer are similar in several important ways. Schiller, as Carlyle, was born of humble parents. He, too, had been destined for the ministry. As Carlyle, Schiller had experienced religious doubt even while he insisted upon the importance of religious conviction. And both were burdened with obscure physical ills throughout their lives. The lives of most of Carlyle's heroes contain parallels to his own.

Finally, Carlyle's interest in literature rarely extended very far beyond the content of the writer's life and the content of what he wrote. He was not greatly interested in literature as art, but rather in what he perceived to be the writer's moral statement. Schiller maintains the same high purpose for literature that Carlyle later finds to be characteristic of the "Hero as Poet" in *Heroes and Hero-Worship*. "As Schiller viewed it," he writes, "genuine Literature includes the essence of philosophy, religion, art; whatever speaks to the immortal part of man. . . . The treasures of Literature are thus celestial, imperishable, beyond all price: . . ." (*Schiller*, 200 - 201).

But, in spite of similarities of statement and attitude, the tone of *Schiller* differs widely from that of Carlyle's later works. *Schiller* contains little of the moral indignation that becomes characteristic of Carlyle's later writing.

## II   Oliver Cromwell's Letters and Speeches

The dogma of the hero dominates *Oliver Cromwell's Letters and Speeches.*[3] In this work, published in 1845, Carlyle perfected the biographical pattern suggested in *The Life of Schiller*. Cromwell satisfied all the requirements for a hero of action. He had perfected his moral development through soul crisis. His aims were frankly religious in nature. His reforms were directed to the establishment of a society that would have for its chief law and chief authority the will of God. Furthermore, he believed that his actions had the sanction of divinity. If Cromwell lacked the intellectual capabilities of Carlyle's poet-heroes, he had, almost to a fault, their high-minded devotion to the cause of truth and goodness.

Carlyle's plan to portray the life of a man by an edition of letters and speeches was not original nor, at this time, even unusual. The method had been developed in the eighteenth century as a result of scholarly desire for accuracy, influenced perhaps by the popularity of the epistolary novel. Mason's *Memoirs of Thomas Gray* (1775) and Moore's *Life of Lord Byron* (1830) had employed letters almost to the exclusion of other types of material. Boswell and Lockhart had used letters freely in their biographies. Carlyle's contribution to the method was his interpretation of the documents.

His objectives in this biography were two: he will correct those writers whose work stood between the public and a clear understanding of his hero, and he will provide a sympathetic interpretation of Cromwell's character and actions. The situation was one in which Carlyle had little difficulty. He had no difficulty establishing a sympathetic understanding for a man whose ideals were approximations of his own, and he would rely upon Cromwell's letters and speeches as true detail upon which to base his interpretations. Conditions were so favorable that he weakened his reader's sympathy for his position by attacks on earlier commentators, whom he identified collectively as "Dryasdust." Whatever the misdeeds of "Dryasdust" in regard to Cromwell's life, all the faults that Carlyle attributed to him are rooted in his conviction that earlier commentators lacked sympathy for Cromwell because they represented the godless reason of the eighteenth century. Here as elsewhere, Carlyle's religious convictions dominate his approach to his writing.

In *Cromwell*, his religious purpose finds so much to admire that it appears again and again. He writes, "At least, it is with Heroes and God-inspired men that I, for my part, would far rather converse, in what dialect soever they speak! Great, ever fruitful; profitable for reproof, for encouragement, for building-up in manful purposes and works, are the words of those that in their day were men" (*OC*, II, 77). He is careful to emphasize the religious motivation of the English revolution so that no one might believe that because he championed Cromwell, he also championed democratic tendencies. He asks his reader "Not to imagine that it was Constitution, 'Liberty of the people to tax themselves,' Privilege of Parliament, Triennial or Annual Parliaments, or any modification of these sublime Privileges now waxing somewhat faint in our admirations, . . ." (I, 81) that brought about the conflict. And he reminds him to bear in mind that "Our ancient Puritan Reformers were, as all Reformers that will ever much benefit this Earth are always, inspired by a Heavenly Purpose" (81 - 82).

Through his desire to brighten Cromwell's tarnished name, Carlyle became the first of Cromwell's nineteenth century biographers to see in the Lord Protector something far greater than a ruthless warrior. To Carlyle he is the ideal man of action. His great ability is the reduction of chaos to order in the field of government. Great perceptions, tremendous soul struggles are not found in his life, for he was neither a *Vates*-prophet nor a *Vates*-poet; nevertheless, he had been, as all true heroes, perfected by suffering before he attained his clear vision of truth. The following passage is central to Carlyle's understanding of his subject.

In those years it must be that Sr. Simcott, Physician in Huntingdon, had to do with Oliver's hypochondriac maladies. He told Sir Philip Warwick, unluckily specifying no date, or none that has survived, "he had often been sent for at midnight"; Mr. Cromwell for many years was very "splenetic" (spleen-struck), often thought he was just about to die, and also "had fancies about the Town Cross." Brief intimation; of which the reflective reader may make a great deal. Samuel Johnson too had hypochondrias; all great souls are apt to have,—and to be in thick darkness generally, till the eternal ways and the celestial guiding-stars disclose themselves, and the vague Abyss of Life knit itself up into Firmaments for them. Temptations in the Wilderness, Choices of Hercules, and the like, in succinct or loose form, are appointed for every man that will assert a soul in himself and be a man. Let

Oliver take comfort in his dark sorrows and melancholies. The quantity of sorrow he has, does it not mean withal the quantity of *sympathy* he has, the quantity of faculty and victory he shall yet have? Our sorrow is the inverted image of our nobleness. The depth of our despair measures what capability and height of claim we have to hope. Black smoke as of Tophet filling all your universe, it can yet by true heart-energy become *flame*, and brilliancy of Heaven. (50 - 51)

The doubt, heartbreak, and soul struggle in Cromwell's life are not discussed in detail. Carlyle looked into the facts available, found that Cromwell was a hypochondriac, and discovered in his hero's life a period of spiritual struggle similar to his own. Cromwell, as Samuel Johnson or Carlyle, emerges victorious from his crisis with a clear view of the nature of the universe. "It is therefore in these years, undated by History," Carlyle writes, "that we must place Oliver's clear recognition of Calvinistic Christianity; what he, with unspeakable joy, would name his Conversion; his deliverance from the jaws of Eternal Death. Certainly a grand epoch for a man: properly the one epoch; the turning-point which guides upwards, or guides downwards, him and his activity forevermore" (51). Carlyle does not let his thesis drift. He is determined to certify Cromwell as an agent of divine will.

Finally, the hero must be perfected by conquering ambition. Carlyle had already pointed out that ambition was the great flaw in the characters of Scott and Napoleon, and he was convinced that ambition is one of the traits of tyranny. In the case of Cromwell, Carlyle could not find the details that established *entsagen* in his hero's life, but he could determine that Cromwell was a farmer until the age of forty. At that age a man does not suddenly become ambitious, according to Carlyle. At every opportunity, Cromwell's letters are interpreted as the expressions of a man of devout nature, and on this point Carlyle's evidence seems to be conclusive, for the letters certainly seem to be written by a man who lived to do only what he thought to be the will of God. The passage that follows is a portion of a letter that was written by Cromwell; the interpretation of the letter is characteristic of Carlyle's method.

Truly no poor creature hath more cause to put himself forth in the cause of his God than I. I have had plentiful wages beforehand; and I am sure I shall never earn the least mite. The Lord accept me in His Son, and give me to walk in the light,—and give us to walk in the light, as He is the light! He it is that enlighteneth our blackness, our darkness, I dare not say, He hideth

His face from me. He giveth me to see light in His light. One beam in a dark place hath exceeding much refreshment in it:—blessed be His Name for shining upon so dark a heart as mine! You know what my manner of life hath been. Oh, I lived in and loved darkness, and hated light; I was a chief, the chief of sinners. This is true: I hated godliness, yet God had mercy on me. O the riches of His mercy! Praise Him for me;—pray for me, that He who hath begun a good work would perfect it in the day of Christ. (101)

Drawing upon his principle of sympathetic insight and upon his own spiritual experience for the management of his tone, Carlyle develops his metaphor of spirit fully in his interpretation of Cromwell's letter.

O modern reader, dark as this Letter may seem, I will advise thee to make an attempt towards understanding it. There is in it a "tradition of humanity" worth all the rest. Indisputable certificate that man once had a soul; that man once walked with God,—his little Life a sacred island girdled with Eternities and Godhoods. . . . Yes, there is a tone in the soul of this Oliver that holds of the Perennial. With a noble sorrow, with a noble patience, he longs towards the mark of the prize of the high calling. He, I think, had chosen the better part. The world and its wild tumults,—if they will but let him alone! Yet he too will venture, will do and suffer for God's cause, if the call come. What man with better reason? He hath had plentiful wages beforehand; snatched out of darkness into marvellous light: he will never earn the least mite. Annihilation of self; *Selbsttödtung*, as Novalis calls it; casting yourself at the footstool of God's throne, "To live or to die for ever; as Thou wilt, not as I will." (103)

Thus does Carlyle infer Cromwell's renunciation of things worldly from Cromwell's own words. To his own satisfaction, at least, Carlyle has established the death of self-interest in Cromwell's character. From this point on, Cromwell is the agent of God. His actions are inspired not of his own, but of God's will. His successes are the manifestation of the power of God. In the name of God, victory after victory falls into the hands of the farmer-patriot, now captain, major, colonel, general, in the parliamentary forces. Finally, the protectorship itself, with which he was presented on December 12, 1653, is the physical manifestation of God's mysterious might.

Cromwell's assumption of the highest position in Puritan England leads Carlyle to the consideration of power and the use of it. He writes, "The love of 'power,' if thou understand what to the manful heart 'power' signifies, is a very noble and indispensable love" (III, 83). All of Carlyle's heroes are, to greater or lesser degree, agents of power; but they have removed themselves from charges of ambition and ruthlessness by annihilation of self. In Carlyle's eyes, they represent the will of God. "Occasion God-sent," he writes, "rushes storming on amid the world's events, swift, perilous; like a whirlwind, like fleet lightning-steed: manfully thou shalt clutch it by the mane, and vault into thy seat on it, and ride and guide there, thou! Wreck and ignominious overthrow, if thou have dared when the Occasion was *not* thine; everlasting scorn to thee if thou dare not when it is . . ." (84). Carlyle's love of power is the love of God. Ventures not supported by divine will are frustrated, ending in chaos and moral despair. His particular view of power, as expressed above, takes it from the hands of those who would use it for their own purposes. Successful ventures, historical outcomes, terrible though they may be, are empowered by divine will. The ways of Carlyle's God were dark and mysterious, indifferent to humanistic values. But there is nothing about them that violates the Calvinistic faith in which he was reared. Cromwell fills Carlyle's demand for a God-ordained hero and serves, at the same time, as evidence of the favor with which God rewards his agents.

Except for its length, *Cromwell* conforms closely to Carlyle's principles of biography. It is said to have revised its readers' estimates of Cromwell; a reading of it today can do much to revise the current understanding of Carlyle's literary purpose.

## III  The Life of John Sterling

Readers have sometimes expressed surprise that Carlyle could have written *The Life of John Sterling*, for this biography of a young friend contains few of the tones or stylistic traits that characterize his writing in general. But *Sterling* was written to correct the injustices of Archdeacon Julius Hare's unfavorable assessment of the man, not as a work intended to support Carlyle's lifelong thesis of divine participation in human events through the agency of the hero. Published in 1851, when Carlyle was fifty-six years of age, *Sterling* (along with his reminiscences of Edward Irving, Lord Jeffrey, and Jane Welsh Carlyle, written fifteen years later) stands as a vivid refutation to critics who argue that sometime after 1840 Carlyle became an irresponsible, probably mad, advocate of brute force.[4]

Turning from the manner in which he customarily promotes his thesis, Carlyle becomes considerably more moderate in his expectations and accomodating in his judgments. At the same time, he remains faithful to his principles for writing biography. Every chapter of *Sterling* reveals his "seeing-eye" and "loving heart." He writes with the confidence of one who thoroughly understands the nature of his subject. And, although he concedes that Sterling's life is not important enough to merit a biography, he neither demeans his subject nor hides his inadequacies. Pointing out that the most serious flaw in Sterling's character is his lack of persistence, Carlyle writes, "In fact, however splendid and indubitable Sterling's qualifications for a parliamentary life, there was that in him withal which flatly put a negative on any such project. He had not the slow steady-pulling diligence which is indispensable in that, as in all important pursuits and strenuous human competitions whatsoever" (*Sterling*, 42). Yet, even as he identifies Sterling's weaknesses, he praises his friend's real worth. "No pleasanter companion," he writes, "I suppose had any of them. So frank, open guileless, fearless, a brother to all worthy souls whatsoever. Come when you might, here is he open-hearted, rich in cheerful fancies, in grave logic, in all kinds of bright activity" (46). Carlyle has avoided the "mealy-mouthed" quality, the partial honesty, that he denounced in his review of Lockhart's *Life of Scott* in 1838. The straightforward praise and blame found in *Sterling* certifies the compatibility of sympathy and truth as effective principles for biographical writing.

An important difference that distinguishes *Sterling* from Carlyle's other biographical writing is his personal knowledge of his subject. Carlyle's personal knowledge of the details of Sterling's life is transformed to vivid biographical narrative by his sympathetic treatment. Few readers deny the comparative superiority of "Burns" and *Sterling* to "Novalis" and *Schiller*. Carlyle was aware of how personal knowledge enlivened his writing, as can be seen in his great eagerness to study all things connected with his subjects. He studied their portraits with great care. He visited the battlefields upon which they fought and the places they frequented whenever he could arrange to do so. He describes the natural setting in which events take place and even the weather of the season of the year, if he can gather information about it. He sought out the believable anecdote in preference to the cold fact. That he found sensual personal involvement necessary for his writing explains the emotional and editorial intrusions of his personality into what he writes better than do charges of irresponsibility, physical illness, or psychological disorder. Commonly treated as a Victorian and judged by Victorian standards, Carlyle comes into focus best when he is seen in a romantic context.

The style of Carlyle's prose is almost always romantic when he is writing at his best. The following description of his first meeting with Sterling is a typical example of the romantic quality of much that he wrote. "A loose, Careless-looking, thin figure, in careless dim costume, sat, in a lounging posture, carelessly and copiously talking. I was struck with the kindly but restless swift-glancing eyes, which looked as if the spirits were all out coursing like a pack of merry eager beagles, beating every bush" (105). The personal point of view, the connotative language and the associations it brings to mind, the open sentences, and the total impression of all these things together betray the romantic writer at ease with his language. A second example, describing the end of a farewell party given Sterling just before one of his trips to Italy in search of health, demonstrates the quality of Carlyle's personal involvement with his subject. Here the author's participation in the event is used to establish a tone of foreboding for Sterling's situation.

One of the liveliest recollections I have, connected with the *Anonymous Club*, is that of once escorting Sterling, after a certain meeting there, which I had seen only towards the end, and now remember nothing of,—except that, on breaking-up, he proved to be encumbered with a carpet-bag, and could not at once find a cab for Knightsbridge. Some small bantering hereupon, during the instants of embargo. But we carried his carpet-bag, slinging it on my stick, two or three of us alternately, through dusty vacant streets, under the gaslights and the stars, towards the surest cab-stand; still jesting, or pretending to jest, he and we, not in the mirthfulest manner; and had (I suppose) our own feelings about the poor Pilgrim, who was to go on the morrow, and had hurried to meet us in this way, as the last thing before leaving England. (160)

The passage illustrates the nature of Carlyle's skill at its very best. On the literal level, Sterling is simply leaving England for a trip to Italy in search of health. But given the context of the paragraph, it communicates considerably more information. Sterling has left the church, and Carlyle has informed his reader that ill health was the external cause. The deeper cause was spiritual (102 - 103). Connotation and association convey extensional meaning. Those attending the farewell gathering at the Anonymous Club are given no names. Sterling is identified as a pilgrim, not as a traveler. The event takes place at night when the streets are deserted, dusty, and artificially lighted. Transportation cannot be found, and the friends carry Sterling's burden, his want of a clear faith. Knightsbridge, the pilgrim's immediate destination, will hopefully prove to be a means to enable him, the pilgrim knight, to a day when he will find health in spirit and in body. The failing attempts at light-hearted banter and the expression "poor pilgrim" reveal the lack of hope the friends place in Sterling's pilgrimage.

In *Sterling,* Carlyle does not use the tone that characterizes the *Latter-Day Pamphlets.* Here, Carlyle's tone is carefully subdued, but he leaves no doubt in the reader's mind about his point of view. *Sterling* is the spiritual biography of a man who has turned away from his faith to follow the Kantean teachings of Coleridge. Though he does not reflect deeply about the well-being of his soul, he is concerned with the issues of the day. He becomes involved in a plot to restore exiled Spanish republicans to power and promotes the participation of Robert Boyd, his cousin, in the event. He himself remains behind for reasons of health. The venture, called the Torrijos affair, was a failure; and Boyd and his companions were captured and executed.

The tragedy turns Sterling's thoughts inward. He regards himself responsible for his cousin's death.

A great remorseful misery had come upon him. Suddenly, as with a sudden lightning-stroke, it had kindled into conflagration all the ruined structure of his past life; such ruin had to blaze and flame round him, in the painfulest manner, till it went out in black ashes. His democratic philosophies, and mutinous radicalisms, already falling doomed in his thought, had reached their consumation and final condemnation here. It was all so rash, imprudent, arrogant, all that; false, or but half-true; inapplicable wholly as a rule of noble conduct;—and it has ended *thus.* Wo on it! Another guidance must be found in life, or life is impossible!—(90)

The use of catastrophe to effect change in human perception is not original with Carlyle. Greek dramatists used it to measure the stature of their heroes. Shakespeare used it to effect changes in the perception of his heroes. Evangelical preachers used it to demonstrate the effectiveness of righteousness against its onslaught. Carlyle's use of it places him somewhere between the artist and the preacher.

The catastrophe that brings about Sterling's soul crisis demonstrates the inadequacy of his moral position and, artistically, provides a dramatic context for the narration of his life. His soul crisis threw him into the arms of the Church of England, where for eight months he served as curate to Julius Charles Hare, rector of Herstmonceux and later his biographer. At the end of this time, Sterling resigned his position, using his ill heath as an excuse. Sterling's period in the church is to Carlyle illuminative of his spiritual development and of the influences operating upon it. Following his resignation, Sterling endures the vicissitudes of the "centre of indifference." His consumptive condition intensifies his problems in finding work. The result of many trials and errors was that Sterling finally turned to writing as the only work he could do. His soul crisis is over. As yet, however, he has no distinct belief, no belief in Christianity, asserts Carlyle; but he is a sincere young man who struggles toward his goal. By the time he achieved order in his spiritual life, his body had weakened beyond recovery. Sterling died without achieving his goal. His life was, Carlyle writes, "A tragic history, as all histories are; yet a gallant, brave and noble one, as not many are" (266).

Though Sterling was not destined for success, his life Carlyle believes, provides helpful instruction, particularly for the young.

In Sterling's Writings and Actions, were they capable of being well read, we consider that there is for all true hearts, and especially for young noble seekers, and strivers towards what is highest, a mirror in which some shadow of themselves and of their immeasurably complex arena will profitably present itself. Here also is one encompassed and struggling even as they now are. This man also had said to himself, not in mere Catechism-words, but with all his instincts, and the question thrilled in every nerve of him, and pulsed in every drop of his blood: "What is the chief end of man? Behold, I too would live and work as beseems a denizen of this Universe, a child of the Highest God. By what means is a noble life still possible for me here? Ye Heavens and thou Earth, oh, how?"—The history of this long-continued prayer and endeavour, lasting in various figures for near forty years, may now and for some time coming have something to say to men! (268)

The passage argues, first and foremost, an idealistic seriousness of purpose for man and offers Carlyle's biography of Sterling as prac-tical aid in the pursuit of a noble life. " 'Why write the Life of Sterling?' " he concludes, "I imagine I had a commission higher than the world's, the dictate of Nature herself, to do what now is done" (268).

## IV  *Ancillary Sketches in* Sterling

Carlyle's ability to write miniature portraits is as great as that of any other writer in the nineteenth century. Several miniatures of men who were important in Sterling's life frame Carlyle's biography. The best include sketches of Edward Sterling, John's father; Torrijos, the Spanish exile, and his companions; and the poet Coleridge, whose teaching dominated Sterling's thoughts at a critical point in his life. The sketch of Coleridge is an accurate and sympathetic treatment of a man Carlyle never really liked. In a vivid picture of the poet, Carlyle emphasizes traits of Coleridge just enough to impress them upon the reader's mind. As usual Carlyle treats the spiritual nature of his subject.

A sublime man; who, alone in those dark days, had saved his crown of spiritual manhood; escaping from the black materialisms, and revolutionary deluges, with "God, Freedom, Immortality" still his: a king of men. The practical intellects of the world did not much heed him, or carelessly reckoned him a metaphysical dreamer: but to the rising spirits of the young generation he had this dusky sublime character; and sat there as a kind of *Magus*, girt in mystery and enigma; his Dodoma oakgrove (Mr. Gilman's house at Highgate) whispering strange things, uncertain whether oracles or jargon. (53)

Although Carlyle failed to foresee the influence Coleridge would have on later times, what he writes of Coleridge is not unjust. A later passage, more ambiguously drawn, points to traits that make Coleridge an unsuitable mentor for Sterling.

The good man, he was now getting old, towards sixty perhaps; and gave you the idea of a life that had been full of sufferings; a life heavy-laden, half-vanquished, still swimming painfully in seas of manifold physical and other bewilderment. Brow and head were round, and of massive weight, but the face was flabby and irresolute. The deep eyes, of a light hazel, were as full of sorrow as of inspiration; confused pain looked mildly from them, as in a kind of mild astonishment. The whole figure and air, good and amiable otherwise, might be called flabby and irresolute; expressive of weakness under possibility of strength. He hung loosely on his limbs, with knees bent, and stooping attitude; in walking, he rather shuffled than decisively stept; and a lady once remarked, he never could fix which side of the garden walk would suit him best, but continually shifted, in corkscrew fashion, and kept trying both. A heavy-laden, high aspiring and surely much-suffering man. (54)

Here Carlyle fits his picture of Coleridge into his larger purpose in
the life of Sterling. Without belittling Coleridge's spirit, Carlyle in-
troduces physical traits that convince the reader that the great poet
was a guide of doubtful value for a man like Sterling. The portraits
of men who influenced Sterling contribute greatly to the total attractiveness of *The Life of John Sterling*.

### CHAPTER 8

# The Histories:
## The French Revolution, Heroes and Hero-Worship, Past and Present

ALTHOUGH social events and conditions are the primary concern of *The French Revolution* (1837), *Heroes and Hero-Worship* (1841), and *Past and Present* (1843), these three works are solidly built on biographical material in close harmony with Carlyle's understanding of the nature of history and society. He believed that history is the essence of many biographies, and he also believed that history is the biography of the hero. Underlying these apparently contradictory statements is Carlyle's conviction that history is a function of divine law and that the physical conditions of society are indicators of the spiritual health of its people.

## I  The French Revolution

The French Revolution is an event that lends itself to Carlyle's interpretation of it as the only possible result of falsity and disbelief. The philosophical scepticism of the intellectuals, the poverty and ignorance of the lower classes, the selfish incompetence of the ruling class, and the faithlessness of the clergy are in his eyes responsible for its occurrence and its destructive violence. His history is an elaborate illustration of his conviction that human events are directly related to the laws of God. Because France is Godless, she must suffer. "Ye and your fathers have sown the wind, ye shall reap the whirlwind. Was it not, from of old, written: *The wages of sin is death*."[1] Carlyle blames the rationalism and the scepticism of the eighteenth century for the final destruction of faith, but the responsibility for violent revolution must be shared by all classes of society.

True rulers, true followers, and true faith would have removed the cause for violence. "Shall we say, then: Wo to Philosophism, that it destroyed Religion, what it called 'extinguishing the abomination (*écraser l'infame*)'? Wo rather to those that made the Holy an abomination, and extinguishable; wo to all men that live in such a time of world-abomination and world-destruction (58)." Every sham and falsity in French society predicates revolutionary chaos. Thus, the great antagonist in Carlyle's history is spiritual corrosion, which he identifies as "hydra-headed" chaos. In all France can be found no man with the spiritual vitality to vanquish it.

Of the men who struggle to make order of the terrible chaos, Mirabeau comes the closest to being the natural king of France. Had he lived, he might have brought the revolution under control. In the eyes of Carlyle, he was qualified to lead France in all respects but one: Mirabeau did not have the requisite spiritual qualities. When he died, destroyed by his efforts to control the revolution, France plunges into the depths of anarchy and violence.

Although Mirabeau comes closest to fulfilling Carlyle's requirements for the hero, literally dozens of lesser men and women are vividly described, always with an eye to their moral qualities. Louis, the weak king, Lafayette, the single-minded, Robespierre, the sea-green incorruptible, are only a few among the many. No picture is too small if it helps depict the lesson that Carlyle wished to teach. Pitted against all the leaders of France is the great antagonist, the "hydra-headed chaos." It sneers in the decadence of the court, screams in the madness of the mobs, and cowers in the faces of its victims. It stalks through the three volumes of Carlyle's history, bloody and irresistible, because France can produce no hero to constrain it; and no hero can constrain it because "In every man is some obscure feeling that his position, oppressive or else oppressed, is a false one" (79).

The nobility once "did actually *lead* the world. . . . But now, when so many Looms, improved Ploughshares, Steam-Engines, and Bills of Exchange have been invented; and, for battle-brawling itself, men hire Drill-Sergeants at eighteenpence a-day,—what mean these goldmantled Chivalry Figures, walking there 'in black-velvet cloaks,' in high-plumed 'hats of a feudal cut'? Reeds shaken in the wind!" (146). The clergy is "an anomalous mass of men. . . . They were once a Priesthood, interpreters of Wisdom, revealers of the Holy that is in Man; a true *Clerus* (or Inheritance of God on Earth): but now?—They pass silently, . . . and none cries,

God bless them!" (147 - 48). The intellectuals write pamphlets and
debate irregular verbs. The shepherds have strayed, and the flock is
aimless and discontented. "They are not tended, they are only
regularly shorn. . . . Untaught, uncomforted, unfed; to pine
stagnantly in thick obscuration, in squalid destitution and obstruc-
tion: this is the lot of the millions; . . ." (13). Moral disorder has
undermined the entire society, and chaos in the guise of
*sanscullotism* stalks the land. "It too came from God; for has it not
*been?* From of old, it is written, are His goings forth; in the great
Deep of things; fearful and wonderful now as in the beginning: in
the whirlwind also He speaks; and the wrath of men is made to
praise Him" (213). In Carlyle's eyes, the events of the French
Revolution rest firmly on moral disorder.

He believed that the revolution was an expression of the "way of
the Eternal as mirrored in the world of Time." Once it begins it will
move from terror to terror until the causes giving rise to it disappear. The execution of the king, the flight of the nobility, and the
widely spread slaughter and destruction cannot stem its course. By
its very nature, revolution destroys its enemies and leaders alike.
Louis, Danton, Mirabeau, Robespierre move toward fated ends, as
do Girondist, Jacobin, and Anti-Jacobin. But there were men who
struggled against the forces of chaos, and Carlyle gives them the
sympathy and credit that he believes they merit. In 1837, when
Carlyle published *The French Revolution*, he had clearly described
the nature of the hero he looked to for the resolution of social
problems. That hero was a man of deep spiritual insight and great
moral strength who had attained his nature through suffering that
purified his vision and certified his selflessness. No such hero
appeared during the French Revolution. Indeed, the French Revolution would not have occurred had a hero of divine order lived in
France at the time, for revolution was the outgrowth of lengthy and
widely spread spiritual disorder. The incomplete and flawed personalities of the revolution rise to prominence only to meet destruction because of their imperfections. Danton, Marot, Robespierre,
Chabray, Lafayette, and many others struggle with the chaos of
their day, but fail.

Carlyle is at his best in his vignettes of those involved in the
historic struggle. Once he has described the nature and the involvement of the individual, he summarizes the personality with a single,
characterizing word or phrase. Lafayette, the single-minded;
Robespierre, the sea-green incorruptible; Mirabeau, the world

compeller, become familiars to the reader through their often repeated epithets. Each character fails in his individual struggle with chaos because of moral flaws, but of all the flawed heroes, Mirabeau comes closest to Carlyle's requirements. "Which of these Six Hundred individuals," he asks, ". . . might one guess would become their *king?* . . . It is *Gabriel Honoré Riquetti de Mirabeau*, the world compeller; man-ruling Deputy of Aix!" (137). He sees Mirabeau as "a fiery fuliginous mass" and as "a burning mountain blazing heaven-high;" but after twenty-three months, he lies "all hollow" and "cold forever!" (140 - 41). As the others, Mirabeau proves not to have the necessary spiritual strength to tame the revolution; and when he dies, exhausted from his efforts to hold the nation together, France tumbles into the depths of anarchy.

Carlyle's history of the French Revolution is vivid, dramatic and personal. Of Robespierre's death, he writes, "At the foot of the scaffold, they stretched him on the ground till his turn came. Lifted aloft, his eyes again opened; caught the bloody axe. Samson wrenched the coat off him; wrenched the dirty linen from his jaw: the jaw fell powerless, there burst from him a cry;—hideous to hear and see" (III, 285 - 86). The forces of the revolution that oppose the flawed heroes are impersonal, usually faceless and nameless, agents of idleness, hunger, injustice, and vice.

Carlyle's attractiveness as a historian lies in his interest in the individual, his conviction that life is a struggle to the death with the forces of chaos, and his ability to express his concerns in vivid, descriptive language. His purpose in writing is frankly didactic. He believed that history is a text to be read as divine gospel. Man could learn to avoid the penalty of immorality and self-interest by a study of the practical working of the laws of God. His didacticism, expressed time and again throughout *The French Revolution,* dominates the conclusion of the work. "Meanwhile we will hate Anarchy as Death, which it is; . . . Know this also, that out of a World of Unwise nothing but an Unwisdom can be made. Arrange it, constitution-build it, sift it through the ballot-boxes as thou wilt, it is and remains an Unwisdom, . . ." (315). Equating disorder, anarchy, and revolution with a fall from belief in the divine, Carlyle wrote *The French Revolution* as a demonstration to England and to the world of the terrors that befall the society that turns away from true belief.

## II   Heroes and Hero-Worship

The six lectures that make up the work *On Heroes and Hero-Worship and the Heroic in History* were delivered as a series in the spring of 1840. In the course of these lectures, eleven personalities were discussed, each of which was presumably representative of the hero or the heroic under conditions necessary to maintain the law of God. The studies are written, not to shed light upon the personality of the subject, but to forward Carlyle's own theory of the capabilities and function of the gifted man in society. Making an effort to present an evolutionary picture of the role of the hero in different societies and in different ages, Carlyle begins his series with Odin, who represents the hero as divinity. Mahomet, representing the hero as prophet, follows. Dante and Shakespeare are the poet-heroes, and Luther and Knox represent the hero as priest. Johnson, Rousseau, and Burns are the heroes as men of letters. Cromwell and Napoleon are the heroes as king.

Throughout *Heroes and Hero-Worship*, Carlyle's discussion is limited to a single aspect of the personality, the spiritual, which he believes brings about the distinguishing feature of his subjects. "The thoughts they had were the parents of the actions they did; their feelings were the parents of their thoughts: . . . it was the unseen and spiritual in them that determined the outward and actual;—their religion, as I say, was the great fact about them. . . . That once known well, all is known" (*HW*, 3). In Carlyle's view, religion is difficult to distinguish from historical or biographical studies because a man's life is his act of worship, his statement of faith. Carlyle's unorthodox view of religion is interfused with a type of pantheism that identifies all forces within nature with the divine. "This Universe, ah me—what could the wild man know of it; what can we yet know?" he writes. "That it is a Force, and thousandfold Complexity of Forces; a Force which is *not we*. . . . Force, Force, everywhere Force; we ourselves a mysterious Force in the centre of that" (8). Carlyle finds all that is material to be the manifestation of divine will.

Such being Carlyle's view of matter, his hero becomes quite simply that man who can perceive the force that activates the universe and separates it from its visable appearance with which it clothes itself. The clarity with which a man can make this distinction establishes his status as a hero, and the sureness with which his fellow men can grasp and accept his feat determines their status as hero worshippers.

Carlyle does not modify his position concerning the nature of his hero or of those that follow him. He does, however, recognize that each age, if it is not to fall into complete chaos and destruction, turns to that hero most necessary for its preservation. Because all heroes are perceivers of the emblematic nature of matter, the individual hero resembles heroes of all ages. But heroes of any age are figures of divine power, whatever their differences. Understanding the nature of the universe, recognizing that the power within themselves has the same source as the power found within all things, they affirm, rather than struggle with, the divine will. Carlyle did not proclaim a power philosophy precisely. For, in his mind, power was not brute strength. It was the law of the universe. It was the beautiful, the mysterious, the divine. His heroes are not the heroes of myth or anthropology; they are the more perfectly attuned beings in a divine creation.

*Heroes and Hero-Worship* is not, therefore, a perverse book that justifies willful actions or actions of destructive violence. It is a book that rests upon the conviction that the law of God is the law of life, that "The greatest of all Heroes is One—whom we do not name here" (11). Those who find Carlyle's doctrine a bald declaration that "might is right" are inaccurate only to the degree that they leave Carlyle's belief in the ministering "life force" out of their considerations. The man who uses power for its own sake, who uses it perversely or selfishly, will be destroyed by the same power that he abuses. The might embodied in Carlyle's heroes is life preserving and culture preserving.

But if Carlyle's force is life force and if it is as central to his work as it appears to be, how is the reader to understand its nature and function? In his essays, Carlyle asserts that it is indistinguishable from all life, beauty, and truth. In *Sartor Resartus* and the biographical works, he demonstrates the process of gaining the vision of it and the benefits of it through suffering and the death of self. In *The French Revolution*, he shows how the society that has strayed from the worship of it enters into a period of confusion, injustice, and violence. The "death-struggles" of the French Revolution are depictions of the blinding of the "seeing-eye" and the emergence of self-concern expressed in frustration, anger, and isolation when the vision, which all nature embodies, fades from human belief. *Heroes and Hero-Worship* demonstrates how man may recover the vision of life through the agency of the hero. Heroes for Carlyle are the saviors of mankind.

Thus, in the lecture on Odin, Carlyle finds much to admire. Nature is regarded as the revelation of the will of God. Frost, fire, and tempest, the destructive forces of nature, are the elements of chaos against which the sun and summer heat, the life forces, contend. Odin, the chief god of the culture, is a thinking and perceiving hero who was transformed into a god by the gratitude and love of his followers. Though he existed in a dim age, Odin was the light of intellect, the nobleness of heart that gave it what light it had. Carlyle reads the faith of the Norse peoples as a rude but impressive understanding of the nature of the universe.

Carlyle makes the same point in "The Hero as Prophet," his second lecture. Choosing Mahomet as his hero, he finds that the prophet is a sincere man whose message was a true one delivered in all sincerity after a long and faithful struggle toward the good. The prophet sees his world as a visual and tactual manifestation of divine power. In spite of Carlyle's discomfort with Mahomet's warlike propogation of his religion, he asserts that the prophet's faith is a "kind of Christianity" (76). His Koran, he avers, is a good book in harmony with divine decree. Sincere, devout, and committed to his perceptions, his doctrines were to the Arab nations a "birth from darkness into light" (77).

"The Hero as Poet" continues Carlyle's demonstration of the role of the hero in a new context. He suggests examples of heroes as men of letters, who struggled, each in his own way, to express the wonder and the beauty of the life force.

In "The Hero as King," the last lecture, Carlyle points to Cromwell and Napoleon as hero-kings who rose to their positions because of the failure of the "sham" heroes of their times. Democratic movements he understood as "the tools to him who can handle them," a process by which leadership is returned to the hero as the ablest of his time. Any other definition of democracy, he consistently deplored.

Carlyle's hero is a man whose responses are dominated by his personality. In his thinking, he is intuitive rather than logical. In his actions, he is direct and natural rather than conventional. He is oriented to a world of value, rather than to a world of materials or of objective fact. His motivations are internal rather than external. He is individualistic, emotional, and demanding. He is the man who can determine best what to do. His nature brings him in contact with the "Law of the Whole," the "Necessity" of the universe, which he must accept despite the urgings of "flesh-and-blood" or "-vain sorrows and wishes" (56 - 57). Whether the hero appears as god, prophet, or poet depends more upon the needs of society at the time and place of his appearance than upon the particular aptitudes of the hero. The "Hero can be Poet, Prophet, King, Priest or what you will, according to the kind of world that he finds himself born into" (78). Pointing out that the poet was originally called *Vates*, Carlyle regards poet and prophet as essentially of the same nature and distinguishes between the *Vates*-poet and the *Vates*-prophet by noting that the *Vates*-prophet treats the divine mystery from a moral point of view and the *Vates*-poet treats it from an aesthetic point of view. Embracing all things, the life force can be approached through its beauty as well as through its moral law. Dante and Shakespeare, Carlyle's examples of the hero as poet, differ as widely as possible. Dante embodies in his *Divine Comedy* the unseen world of his time, and Shakespeare pictures the outer life that grew from the inner.

"The Hero as Priest," the topic of the fourth lecture, functions as the hero-teacher who leads men from darkness into light. Carlyle sees Luther and Knox doing just that, each in his own way. The hero as priest teaches how all men can become heroes. In contrast, "The Hero as the Man of Letters," his fifth lecture, points out the changing needs of society and suggests that in the nineteenth century the man of letters has undertaken the role once held by the hero-priest. The books written by the hero as man of letters have become our university, our church, and our parliament. Johnson, Rousseau, and Burns, Carlyle's examples of heroes as men of letters, struggle each in his own way to express the wonder and the beauty of the life force. The function of every hero at every time and place is to turn society toward reality. Although he accomodates his ideas of heroes to change, Carlyle insists upon no particular line of development for society and upon no particular type of hero. As old symbols and metaphors for divine truth lose their significance, the hero will cast them away and express the same truth in new forms.

In *Heroes and Hero-Worship*, Carlyle broadens his theory of the hero to include men that he himself did not greatly admire. He had discovered that all ages are not times of song and prophecy. The hero must turn his people always toward the everlasting truths.

### III Past and Present

*Past and Present,* published in 1843, places Carlyle's concern for spiritual leadership in the context of nineteenth century economics, which he then compares to that of the twelfth century. Again Carlyle emphasizes the role of the divine in history, but now he presents it as a riddle of the Sphinx that man must solve or face destruction. "Nature, like the Sphinx, is of womanly celestial loveliness and tenderness; the face and bosom of a goddess, but ending in claws and the body of a lioness."[2] In this book Carlyle's "life force" emerges as transcendental justice, which is also beauty, toward which creation moves. "Towards an eternal centre of right and nobleness, and of that only, is all this confusion tending" (12).

The problems of the nineteenth century, Carlyle believes, are the result of democratic movements, *laissez faire,* and the industrial revolution. The nature of justice, though it is the subject of much of his discourse, is by no means transparent. Carlyle describes it as all things in one, as a transcendental virtue.

If you do not know eternal Justice from momentary Expediancy, and understand in your heart of hearts how Justice, radiant, beneficent, as the all-victorious Light-element, is also in essence, if need be, an all-victorious *Fire*-element, and melts all manner of vested interests, and the hardest iron cannon, as if they were soft wax, and does ever in the long-run rule and reign, and allows nothing else to rule and reign,—you would also talk of impossibility! But it is only difficult, it is not impossible. Possible? It is, with whatever difficulty, very clearly inevitable. (19)

Carlyle's faith in the inevitable nature of justice renders the present confusing and painful to him. He responds to the same conditions that inspired the doctrines of Karl Marx. He is distressed by the poverty and by the decadence that he sees about him, and he also condemns the church and the state for their inability to correct the evils of the time. Carlyle, however, believed in the ethical nature of the universe as Marx did not. Carlyle's "life force" is not the programmed viciousness that critics sometimes picture. In his efforts to put new wine into old bottles, he hangs precariously between fantasy and psychological truth. His cure for social ills is not reform by legislation. Convinced that the universe is moral, he offers moral reform as the cure for any problem. "When a Nation is unhappy, the old Prophet was right and not wrong in saying to it:

Ye have forgotten God, ye have quitted the ways of God, or ye would not have been unhappy" (28).

Moral reform, however, is only the first step. Once man faces moral reality, he will be able to see how far he has strayed into regions of "lawless Chaos." He will then understand that legislation is helpless and that hero worship is the only permament solution to human misery.

To the present Editor, "Hero-worship," as he has elsewhere named it, means much more than an elected Parliament, or stated Aristocracy, of the Wisest; for in his dialect it is the summary, ultimate essence, and supreme practical perfection of all manner of "worship," and true worthships and noblenesses whatsoever. Such blessed Parliament and, were it once in perfection, blessed Aristocracy of the Wisest, god-honoured and man-honoured, he does look for, more and more perfected,—as the topmost blessed practical apex of a whole world reformed from sham-worship, informed anew with worship, with truth and blessedness! He thinks that Hero-worship, done differently in every different epoch of the world, is the soul of all social business among men; that the doing of it well, or the doing of it ill, measures accurately what degree of well-being or of ill-being is in the world's affairs. (34)

As an illustration of his conviction, Carlyle tells how in an age of faith, the monks of St. Edmundsbury select their new abbot. They know "that this Earthly Life and *its* riches and possessions, and good and evil hap, are not intrinsically a reality at all, but *are* a shadow of realities eternal, infinite" (66 - 67). Their faith and their reverence for true worth leads them to the selection of the best man as their abbot. Brother Samson, who is their unconscious choice for the position, fulfills Carlyle's requirements for the hero. He has had trials that have enabled him to attain selflessness. He hates disorder and shoddyness in all things. He is a silent, hardworking, middle-aged man who no longer possesses personal ambition. His appointment as abbot of St. Edmundsbury is yet another illustration of Carlyle's conviction that the universe functions according to divine order.

The king has power of appointment, but the abbey must be satisfied too. When the prior and twelve monks are called before the king for the purpose of selecting the new abbot, Samson is among the twelve representing the abbey. In recognition of his honesty and other virtues, he is the holder of the purse. He also carries a slip of paper on which are written three names chosen by the six most venerable elders of the abbey. Meeting with the king, the monks are asked by him to submit three names of men they will accept as their abbot. The king does not know the three and insists that the delegation submit three more names. Three more names, all men of St. Edmundsbury, are submitted. The king asks for the names of three men who are not members of the abbey. They are presented. Nine names are now on the list, and the problem is to find the best man for the position. After considerable thought, the delegation settles on Samson because he is the most able. No system or method can teach man to choose the hero as ruler. Only hero worship, a love for the true, the worthy, the divine wherever it is found, can lead man to the selection of his rulers. Elections made in any other way result in misgovernment and social misery.

Although Carlyle places the blame for social or personal evil on godlessness, he has a keen eye for reality. He is saddened by the tragedy of a poor Irish widow who establishes her brotherhood to man by infecting seventeen people who had refused to help her. He is outraged to see willing workers unemployed or underpaid; and, in the name of a suffering England, he accuses the rulers of England of misgovernment. "I say," he writes, "*you* were appointed to preside over the Distribution and Apportionment of the Wages of Work done; and to see well that there went no labourer without his hire, were it of money coins, were it of hemp gallows-ropes: that function was yours, and from immemorial time has been; yours, and as yet no other's" (171). Having illustrated man's responsibility to man, he develops his notions of just government along elitist lines. The landed aristocracy must rule with justice or disappear. The working aristocracy "must strike into a new path; must understand that money alone is *not* the representative either of man's success in the world, or of man's duties to man; and reform their own selves from top to bottom, if they wish England reformed" (177). The duty of man to man is more than the "cash nexus." "Plugson of Undershot," the captain of industry, must learn from William, the Norman, who stood by his soldiers after the wars as well as during them. The duty of man to man is terminated only by death.

Carlyle was a careful observer of the great social changes that followed the industrial revolution in England. He observed the displacement of old social structures by those of industry and could see no social stability resulting from them. As the enclosure acts and corn laws forced the population to leave their customary places in an agricultural culture for new ones in an industrial culture, the rate of starvation, drunkenness, and crime increased. Under England's political organization, neither church nor state had any way to assume responsibility for their well-being, and little or no legislation existed for their protection. Gurth, Carlyle's peasant who wore about his neck, a brass collar that identified him as Cedric's thrall, was more secure than many who crowded the industrial market in nineteenth century England. "Liberty?" Carlyle writes; "The true liberty of man . . . were that a wiser man, that any and every wiser man, could, by brass collars, or in whatever milder or sharper way, lay hold of him when he was going wrong and order and compel him to go a little righter" (212). For Carlyle freedom lies only in selecting the law of the universe as the way of life. Not to do so is death.

The liberty of social, political, moral, and religious choice furthered by the development of the industrial revolution was not limited by legislative controls when Carlyle wrote. Viewed from the perspective of the twentieth century, Carlyle's complaints are not without foundation. That he was unable to assess the role of Parliament in the development of legislation to protect freedom from its own excesses is not surprising, for his reading of history as the will of God leads him to doubt the validity of democratic government. His conviction that history is the record of divine will lead him to suspect that changes that brought about suffering would be severely corrected. Thus, he used events from the history of the middle ages as models of justice and man's responsibility to man for his nineteenth century audience.

For those were rugged stalwart ages; . . . Dastards upon the very throne had to be got arrested, and taken off the throne,—by such methods as there were; by the roughest method, if there chanced to be no smoother one! Doubtless there was much harshness of operation, much severity; as indeed government and surgery are often somewhat severe. Gurth, born thrall of Cedric, it is like, got cuffs as often as pork-parings, if he misdemeaned himself; but Gurth did belong to Cedric: no human creature then went about connected with nobody; left to go his way into Bastilles or worse, under *Laissez-faire;* reduced to prove his relationship by dying of typhus-fever! (244 - 45)

But if history is the will of God, the rise of democracy is also the will of God, for it was becoming history too. At first, Carlyle regarded democracy as the punishment of God upon man and nation for atheism and "sham." But when democratic revolutions ended and no new nobility appeared to assume command, he modified his views.

The following passage, often overlooked by critics of Carlyle's harsh judgements, is necessary for the understanding of his position at midlife in 1843.

An actual new Sovereignty, Industrial Aristocracy, real not imaginary Aristocracy, is indispensable and indubitable for us. . . .

But what an Aristocracy; on what new far more complex and cunningly devised conditions than that old Feudal fighting one! For we are to bethink us that the Epic verily is not *Arms and the Man*, but *Tools and the Man*,—an infinitely wider kind of Epic. And again we are to bethink us that men cannot now be bound to men by *brass-collars*,—not at all: that this brass-collar method, in all figures of it, has vanished out of Europe forever-more! Huge Democracy, walking the streets everywhere in its Sack Coat, has asserted so much; irrevocably, brooking no reply! True enough, man *is* forever the "born thrall" of certain men, born master of certain other men, born equal of certain others, let him acknowledge the fact or not. It is un-blessed for him when he cannot acknowledge this fact; . . . How, in con-junction with inevitable Democracy, indispensable Sovereignty is to exist: certainly it is the hugest question ever heretofore propounded to Mankind! (250 - 251)

Carlyle's farewell to the middle ages concludes in paradox. It is not, however, a farewell to his doctrine of the hero or to his doctrine of the life force.

Having acknowledged democracy as a continuing form of government, he supplements his ideas with practical suggestions for the first time. He observes that the army has succeeded, while the church and the courts have failed. The functions of government, he notes, must be carried out by agencies patterned after military organization. "I could conceive an Emigration Service, a Teaching Service, considerable varieties of United and Separate Services, of the due thousands strong, all effective as this Fighting Service is; all doing *their* work, like it;—which work, much more than fighting, is henceforth the necessity of these New Ages we are got into!" (262). He suggests legislation to control the freedom of the industrialist, unrestrained under *laissez faire*. He calls for sanitary regulations, legislation controlling soot and smoke, "baths, free air, a wholesome temperature, ceilings twenty feet high" in mills. He urges the es-tablishment of parks of "a hundred acres or so of free greenfield, with trees on it" for the benefit of children. And above all he insists upon an education bill "to irradicate with intelligence, that is to say, with order, arrangement and all blessedness, the Chaotic, Unintelligent" (265 - 66). He concludes his presentation of possible reforms with an appeal to working men to organize "as a firm regimented mass, with real captains over them" (275). If society ever becomes organized on such principles, he speculates, then perhaps the master worker might find it necessary to grant his workers a share in their united project. "A question arises here: Whether, in some ulterior, perhaps some not far-distant stage of this 'Chivalry of Labour,' your Master-Worker may not find it possible, and needful, to grant his Workers permanent *interest* in his enterprise and theirs?" (281 - 82). His practical suggestions are as close as Carlyle comes to prophetic truth, for most of them have now come into existence. But in his thinking they are at best temporary measures to shore up chaos until the hero can deliver mankind from darkness.

### CHAPTER 9

# The History of Frederick the Great

## I  *The Final Statement*

WHEN *Frederick the Great* was completed in 1865, Carlyle was almost the only literary giant who stood against the views of men like Charles Darwin and Thomas Huxley in a society that was rapidly awakening to the possibilities of the new science. He had changed neither his method nor his philosophy, and in *Frederick the Great* he thundered out his doctrine for the last time at its most easily understandable level.

When Carlyle began his study of Frederick in 1851, he was only fifty-six years old; he was a man in good health and in vigorous control of his mind and body. He was, however, sixty-three years old when the first two volumes were published in 1858; and he was seventy years old before he had finished the work. Altogether, he had spent fourteen years of his life on it.

*Frederick the Great* is too long for the contemporary reader. It was long even in the day that produced three volume novels and two volume lives as the usual thing. Carlyle's criticism of Lockhart's *Life of Scott* for excessive length is quite as valid of his own work, and time has supported his judgment of 1828 against his practice of 1858 - 1865. The objection to the length of Carlyle's work would be less if the length could be found to contribute understanding either to the life of Frederick or to the history of his time. Much of the eight volumes does neither. Page after page of *Frederick the Great* is filled with gossipy anecdote that may have been exciting or significant to the reader of nearly a century ago, but today it is only tiresome. Too many of Carlyle's well-loved details, seen in the light of this age, prove to be merest tittle-tattle about decadent rulers of obsolete governments. *The History of Frederick the Great*, however, is important, if for no other reason, because it is Carlyle's last complete statement of his fundamental beliefs.

Carlyle apparently chose Frederick the Great for the subject of a book late in 1851.[1] At approximately the same time, he had worked out a few remarks on religion in a manuscript that he entitled "Spiritual Optics."[2] The manuscript is as complete an exposition as is preserved of Carlyle's direct statements on the subject of religion; it should be noticed before turning to *Frederick the Great* because it indicates clearly enough that Carlyle's opinions about religion in 1851 were substantially what they had been since 1830. Far from abandoning his Calvinistic religion, Carlyle had managed to put what he knew of science to the use of bolstering up his religious convictions.

The primary conception by rude nations in regard to all great attainments and achievements by men is that each was a miracle and the gift of the gods. Language was taught man by a heavenly power. Minerva gave him the olive, Neptune the horse, Triptolemus taught him agriculture, &c. The effects of *optics* in this strange camera obscura of our existence, are most of all singular! The grand centre of the modern revolution of ideas is even this—we begin to have a notion that all this *is* the effect of optics, and that the intrinsic fact is very different from our old conception of it. Not less "miraculous," not less divine, but with an altogether totally new (or hitherto unconceived) *species* of divineness; . . . a divineness that does not come from Judaea, from Olympus, Asgard, Mount Meru, but is in man himself; in the heart of everyone born of man—a grand revolution, indeed, which is altering our ideas of heaven and earth to an amazing extent in every particular whatsoever. From top to bottom our spiritual world, and all that depends on the same, which means nearly everything in the furniture of our life, outward as well as inward, is, as this idea advances, undergoing change of the most essential sort, is slowly getting "overturned," as they angrily say, which in the sense of being gradually turned over and having its vertex set where its base used to be, is indisputably true, and means a "revolution" such as never was before, or at least since letters and recorded history existed among us never was. The great Galileo, or numerous small Galileos, have appeared in our spiritual world too, and are making known to us that the sun stands still; that as for the sun and stars and eternal immensities, they do not move at all, and indeed have something else to do than dance around the like of us and our paltry little dog-hutch of a dwelling place; that it is we and our dog-hutch that are moving all this while, giving rise to such phenomena; and that if we would ever be wise about our situation we must now attend to that fact. I would fain sometimes write a book about all that, and try to make it plain to everybody. But alas! I find again there is next to nothing to be said about it in words at present—and indeed till lately I had vaguely supposed that everybody understood it, or at least understood me to mean it, which it would appear that they don't at all.[3]

Carlyle in 1852, it would seem, was tempted to restate the case for man's divinity to a nation that had already entered the age of materialism and religious doubt.

But now, will the favourable reader permit me to suggest to him a fact which, though it has long been present to the consciousness of here and there a meditative individual, has not, perhaps, struck the favourable reader hitherto—that with the inward eyesight and the spiritual universe there is always, and has always, been the same game going on. Precisely a similar game, to infer motion of your own when it is the object seen that moves; and rest of your own with menadic storming of all the gods and demons; while it is yourself with the devilish and divine impulses that you have, that are going at express train speed! I say the Galileo of this, many small Galileos of this have appeared some time ago—having at length likewise collected (with what infinitely greater labour, sorrow, and endurance than your material Galileo needed) the experience necessary for correcting such illusions of the *inner* eyesight in its turn—a crowning discovery, as I sometimes call it, the essence and summary of all the sad struggles and wrestlings of these last three centuries. No man that reflects need be admonished what a pregnant discovery this is; how it is the discovery of discoveries, and as men become more and more sensible of it will remodel the whole world for us in a most blessed and surprising manner. Such continents of sordid delirium (for it is really growing now very sordid) will vanish like a foul Walpurgis night at the first streaks of dawn. Do but consider it. The delirious dancing of the universe is stilled, but the universe itself (what scepticism did not suspect) is still all there. God, heaven, hell, are none of them annihilated for us, any more than the material woods and houses. Nothing that was divine, sublime, demonic, beautiful, or terrible is in the least abolished for us as the poor pre-Galileo fancied it might be; only their mad dancing has ceased, and they are all reduced to dignified composure; any madness that was in it being recognised as our own henceforth.[4]

Froude reports questioning Carlyle concerning the ideas expressed in the manuscript "Spiritual Optics." Carlyle, he writes, told him that the fragment contained his real conviction about the doings of man in the world. Froude believed, and rightly so, that these remarks were the key to Carlyle's mind. In a second manuscript Carlyle expresses his principle of order as well as his idea of history.

Singular what difficulty I have in getting my poor message delivered to the world in this epoch: things I imperatively need still to say.
1.   That all history is a Bible—a thing stated in words by me more than once, and adopted in a sentimental way; but nobody can I bring fairly into it, nobody persuade to take it up practically as a *fact*.

2. Part of the "grand Unintelligible," that we are now learning spiritually too—that the earth *turns,* not the sun and heavenly spheres. One day the spiritual astronomers will find that *this* is the infinitely greater miracle. . . .

3. And flowing out of this, that the work of genius is not *fiction* but fact. How dead are all people to that truth, recognising it in word merely, not in deed at all! Histories of Europe! Our own history! Eheu! If we had any vivacity of soul and could get the old Hebrew spectacles off our nose, should we run to Judea or Houndsditch to look at the doings of the Supreme? Who conquered anarchy and chained it everywhere under their feet? Not the Jews with their morbid imaginations and foolish sheepskin Targums. The Norse with their steel swords guided by fresh valiant hearts and clear veracious understanding, it was *they* and not the Jews. . . .

Old piety was wont to say that God's judgments tracked the footsteps of the criminal; that all violation of the eternal laws, done in the deepest recesses or on the conspicuous high places of the world, was absolutely certain of its punishment. You could do no evil, you could do no good, but a god would repay it to you. . . .

My friend, it well behoves us to reflect how true essentially all this still is: that it continues, and will continue, fundamentally a fact in all essential particulars—its certainty, I say its infallible certainty, its absolute justness, and all the other particulars, the eternity itself included.[5]

Such expressions of his belief in fact as the word of God and in order as the law of God are important because they show that Carlyle did not abandon his early doctrines when he chose Frederick the Great as the subject for his great work. Fragments of Carlyle's writing are not the only evidences to the fact that Carlyle had not lost the religious convictions of his younger years. Moncure D. Conway, who did not meet Carlyle until 1863, was convinced that Carlyle's nature was essentially religious. "Carlyle's was not only an essentially religious mind, but even passionately so. His profound reverence, his ever-burning flame of devout thought, made him impatient of all such substitutes for these as dogmas and ceremonies—the lamps gone out long ago. There was a sort of divine anger that filled him whenever forced to contemplate selfishness and egotism in the guise of humility and faith."[6]

## II   *A Questionable Hero*

But if Carlyle had not abandoned his religious ideals, how could he devote almost fifteen years of his life to a hero such as Frederick the Great? Conway believed that Carlyle was not completely aware of the character of Frederick until after he had started to write the biography.[7] Norwood Young, one of Carlyle's sharpest critics, accepts Conway's view. "The further he went the less did Carlyle appreciate Frederick, but no trace of any change was allowed to appear in the biography. When it had become a question between his own prestige and the truth, he succumbed to temptation."[8] Conway, who published his biography of Carlyle in 1881, had no material available wherewith he could correct his errors. Young, who had no such excuse, can hardly be justified in his. As a matter of fact, Carlyle was aware of Frederick's nature as early as December 23, 1852, when he wrote as follows to his sister in Dumfries:

"Frederick the Great" continues very questionable; nobody yet could say, I should ever fairly *try* to write a Book about him! The sight of actual Germany, with its flat-soled puddlings in the slough of nonsense (quite a different kind of nonsense from ours, but not a whit less genuine) has hurt poor *Fritz* (Freddy) very much in my mind; poor fellow, he too lies deep-buried in the *middenstank* even as Cromwell did; and then he is not half or tenth-part such a man as Cromwell, that one should swim and dive for him in that manner! In fact tho' I have not yet quitted the neighbourhood of Fritz and his old cocked-hat, his fate is very uncertain with me; and every new German *Book* I read about him, my feeling is, All up with Fritz.[9]

As a subject, Frederick had the disadvantage of being morally inferior to Cromwell, but he lived in the century in which it was difficult to live a godly life. Frederick, though not a man possessed of a poetic or a prophetic nature, is presented by Carlyle as being essentially religious. Like Voltaire, to whom Carlyle compares him, Frederick was an unconscious, if not a devoted, tool of God. Frederick's thirst for action was perhaps the only faith possible for his time. In the eyes of Carlyle such a situation was unfortunate, but it was not sufficient reason to eliminate from consideration the man who was the undeniable leader of his century. He felt obliged to state once more his plan for national government. The result is *Frederick the Great*.

Frederick's life, which equated Prussian stability with godliness and justice, illustrated that even though faith could not be attained and even though the greatest heroes could not be found for men to follow, man could live peacefully and perhaps righteously if guided by a principle of order.

To us as to you this immense explosion of democracy in France, and from end to end of Europe, is very remarkable and full of interest. Certainly never in our time was there seen such a spectacle of history as we are now to look at and assist in. I call it very joyful; yet also unutterably sad. Joyful, inasmuch as we are taught again that all mortals do long towards justice and veracity; that no strongest charlatan, no cunningest fox of a Louis Philippe, with his great *Master* to help him, can found a habitation upon lies, or establish a "throne of iniquity"—nay, that he cannot even attempt such a problem in these times any more; which we may take to be blessed news indeed, in the pass we were come to. But, on the other hand, how sad that the news *should* be so *new* (for that is really the vital point of the mischief); that all the world, in its protest against False Government, should find no remedy but that of rushing into no government or anarchy (kinglessness), which I take this republican universal suffragism to inevitably be. Happily they are not disposed to fight, at least not with *swords*, just yet; but abundance of fighting (probably enough in all kinds) one does see in store for them; and long years and generations of weltering confusion, miserable to contemplate, before anything can be *settled* again.[10]

Democracy, born of revolution, forever in Carlyle's mind remained a state of society synonymous with chaos. In the face of European revolutions, Carlyle perceived that if England could not be awakened with the strident teachings of the *Latter-Day Pamphlets*, it might respond to a carefully drawn portrait of the last true king, Frederick the Great, whose ability to create order out of chaos was to Carlyle the most significant thing about him.

Once Carlyle had settled upon his subject, the reading of source materials absorbed most of his time. Two trips to Germany supplied him with the visual details from which he was fond of reconstructing the action for his biographies.[11] Carlyle's method of preparation was unvarying. His chief effort was perfect familiarization with his subject. He used the method throughout his life and was rewarded, in consequence, by the attainment of an unusually dramatic style.

You ask me how I proceed in taking Notes on such occasions. I would very gladly tell you all my methods if I had any; but really I have as it were none. I go into the business with all the intelligence, patience, silence and other gifts and virtues that I have; find that ten times or a hundred times as many could be profitably expended there, and still prove insufficient: and as for plan, I find that every new business requires as it were a new scheme of operations, which amid infinite bungling and plunging unfolds itself at intervals (very scantily, after all) as I get along. The great thing is, Not to stop and break down; to know that *virtue* must not stop because new and ever new drafts upon one's virtue must be honoured!—But as to the special point of taking Excerpts, I think I universally, from habit or otherwise, rather avoid *writing* beyond the very minimum; mark in pencil the very smallest indication that will direct me to the thing again; and on the whole try to keep the whole matter simmering in the living mind and memory rather than laid up in paper bundles or otherwise laid up in the inert way. For this certainly turns out to be a truth: Only what you at last *have living* in your own memory and heart is worth putting down to be printed; this alone has much chance to get into the living heart and memory of other men. And here indeed, I believe, is the essence of all the rules I have ever been able to devise for myself. (*New Letters*, II, 10 - 11)

But the method of composition that Carlyle describes is also responsible for the weakness of his biography. It is difficult to keep a large number of biographical details simmering in the memory at once.

Carlyle's aim in writing the life of Frederick was not to discover and record the details of his life; it was to present Fredrick as what to all appearances he was, a successful king. The book is Carlyle's considered response to the revolutions of 1848. England must have one more warning of the chaos that Carlyle had observed followed revolution and rule by the masses. To find a model king in modern times was no easy task, and one wonders how Carlyle might have done better. Frederick did represent efficient government, and Carlyle found tyranny a lesser evil than chaos. If tyranny were combined with justice, order ruled; and God's will on earth was done. The aim of *Frederick the Great* was to illustrate the benefits arising from just government by a true king. This aim Carlyle accomplished; but, in the meantime, he wrote neither history nor pure biography.

Carlyle's first care in presenting a model king to the reader is to make certain that it is understood that Frederick is not of decadent or of selfish character. Without ever actually affirming Frederick's selflessness, Carlyle describes him in old age in terms that signify that he has attained *entsagen*. He is described in the same way that Carlyle describes men who have devoted their lives to great tasks.

The man is not of godlike physiognomy, any more than of imposing stature or costume: close-shut mouth with thin lips, prominent jaws and nose, receding brow, by no means of Olympian height; head, however, is of long form, and has superlative gray eyes in it. Not what is called a beautiful man; nor yet by all appearance, what is called a happy. On the contrary, the face bears evidence of many sorrows, as they are termed, of much hard labour done in this world; and seems to anticipate nothing but more still coming. Quiet stoicism, capable enough of what joy there were, but not expecting any worth mention; great unconscious and some conscious pride, well tempered with a cheery mockery of humour,—are written on that old face; . . .[12]

And at the outset of his biography Carlyle defines the type of hero with whom he is dealing. Frederick, Carlyle would have the reader know, is by no means a perfect man. Though he is a successful king, the last of the kings of Europe, a true ruler of men,

Friedrich is by no means one of the perfect demigods; and there are various things to be said against him with good ground. To the last, a questionable hero; with much in him which one could have wished not there, and much wanting which one could have wished. But there is one feature which strikes you at an early period of the inquiry, that in his way he is a Reality; that he always means what he speaks; grounds his actions, too, on what he recognises for the truth; and in short, has nothing whatever of the Hypocrite or Phantasm. (*Frederick*, I, 14)[13]

This preview of Frederick's character and appearance as an old man is effective and disarming. Given at once a favorable picture of Carlyle's hero, the reader is conditioned, as it were, to Carlyle's development of Frederick's personality.

## III    Soul-Crisis and Entsagen

Following a foreground of 318 pages in which he traces the history of Prussia and Frederick's ancestors from 928 A.D. to Frederick's time in a series of sharply drawn and sometimes arresting portraits, Carlyle pictures Frederick's youth with careful emphasis upon whatever characteristics of it might contribute to a spiritual crisis, and the first step of which is the seeding of doubt in the boy's mind by forcing religion on him like drill.

And there is another deeper thing to be remarked: the notion of "teaching" religion, in the way of drill-exercise; which is a very strange notion, though a common one, and not peculiar to Noltenious and Friedrich Wilhelm. Piety to God, the nobleness that inspires a human soul to struggle Heavenward, cannot be "taught" by the most exquisite catechisms, or the most industrious preachings and drillings. No; alas, no. Only by far other methods,—chiefly by silent continual Example, silently waiting for the favourable mood and moment, and aided then by a kind of miracle, well enough named "the grace of God,"—can that sacred contagion pass from soul into soul. (424 - 25)

To Frederick's failure to attain religious faith may be added a disordered life, a second characteristic of the spiritual crisis. Like a good novelist, Carlyle writes significantly of Frederick's debauched life.

As for the poor Crown-Prince, whom already his Father did not like, he now fell into circumstances more abtruse than ever in that and other respects. Bad health, a dangerous lingering fit of that, soon after his return home, was one of the first consequences. Frequent fits of bad health, for some years coming; with ominous rumours, consultations of physicians, and reports to the paternal Majesty, which produced small comfort in that quarter. The sad truth, dimly indicated, is sufficiently visible: his life for the next four or five years was "extremely dissolute." Poor young man, he has got into a disastrous course; consorts chiefly with debauched young fellows, as Lieutenants Katte, Keith, and others of their stamp, who lead him on ways not pleasant to his Father, nor comfortable to the Laws of this Universe. Health, either of body or mind, is not to be looked for in his present way of life. The bright young soul, with its fine strengths and gifts; wallowing like a young rhinoceros in the mud-bath:—some say, it is wholesome for a human soul; not we! (II, 119)

With great care Carlyle illustrates the development of Frederick's spiritual crisis as it advances into its final stages and shows, at last, how the youth already at war with "the laws of God" is pushed into open revolt against his father's will by his stubborn nature. The elements of chaos gain ascendency, and Frederick is placed in prison where he is under arrest for attempted desertion. The incident that occasions the crisis is the death of Frederick's friend Katte, who has been condemned for his part in the affair.

And so here Katte comes; cheerful loyalty still beaming on his face, death now nigh. "*Pardonnez-moi, mon cher Katte!*" cried Friedrich in a tone: "Pardon me, dear Katte; O, that this should be what I have done for you!"—"Death is sweet for a Prince I love so well," said Katte, "*La Mort est douce pour un si aimable Prince;*" and fared on,—round angle of the Fortress, it appears; not in sight of Friedrich; who sank into a faint, and had seen his last glimpse of Katte in this world. (341)

Carlyle shows that the shock of Katte's death brought on Frederick's baptism of fire in a reaction quite similar to that ex-

perienced by Sterling when he heard of the death of his cousin and
believed himself responsible for it. The crisis is a basic part of
Carlyle's method of depicting the development of his subject's
character and is consistently used in Carlyle's biographical works.

Friedrich's feelings at this junction are not made known to us by himself in
the least; or credibly by others in any considerable degree. . . . But it is
evident this last phenomenon fell upon him like an overwhelming cataract;
crushed him down under the immensity of sorrow, confusion and despair;
his own death not a theory now, but probably a near fact,—a welcome one
in wild moments, and then anon so unwelcome. Frustrate, bankrupt,
chargeable with a friend's lost life, sure enough he, for one, is: what is to
become of him? Whither is he to turn, thoroughly beaten, foiled in all his
enterprises? Proud young soul as he was: the ruling Powers, be they just, be
they unjust, have proved too hard for him! We hear of tragic vestiges still
traceable of Friedrich, belonging to this time: texts of Scripture quoted by
him, pencil-sketches of his drawing; expressive of a mind dwelling in
Golgothas, and pathetically, not defiantly, contemplating the very worst.
(342 - 43)

As one might expect from a study of prior works, *entsagen* follows
the black depths of despondency occasioned by the death of Katte.
For Frederick as for John Sterling the experience is of a religious
nature. To illustrate this point Carlyle quotes the story of the son of
the man who was the prince's chaplain at this time.

By the Prince's arrangement, my Father, who at first lodged with the Com-
mandant, had to take up his quarters in the room right above the Prince;
who daily, often as early as six in the morning, rapped on the ceiling for
him to come down, and then they would dispute and discuss, sometimes
half-days, long, about the different tenets of the Christian Sects;—and my
Father said, the Prince was perfectly at home in the Polemic Doctrines of
the Reformed (Calvinistic) Church, even to the minutest points. As my
Father brought him proofs from Scripture, the Prince asked him one time,
How he would keep chapter and verse so exactly in his memory? Father
drew from his pocket a little Hand-Concordance, and showed it him as one
help. This he had to leave with the Prince for some days. On getting it
back, he found inside on the fly-leaf, sketched in pencil, what is rather
notable to History,—"the figure of a man on his knees, with two swords
hanging crosswise over his head; and at the bottom these words of Psalm
Seventy-third (verses 25, 26, *Whom have I in Heaven but Thee? And there
is none upon earth that I desire besides thee. My flesh and my heart
fainteth and faileth; but God is the strength of my heart, and my portion
forever.*"—Poor Friedrich, this is a very unexpected pencil-sketch on his

part; but an undeniable one; betokening abstruse night-thoughts and forebodings in the present juncture. (344)

From this point on Carlyle treats his hero as a man who has achieved spiritual maturity. At no time does Carlyle claim for Frederick an approach to the *vates*-prophet or the *vates*-poet; yet Frederick has made a step in that direction. His soul struggle has not lifted him to an exalted level of spiritual effort; it has, however, taught him the necessity of obedience to a higher power than his own desires, to God and order.

## IV    Limitations and Accomplishments

Carlyle at no time assigns to Frederick greater spiritual purpose than he actually had. Discouraging as it must have been to point out serious flaws in his model king. Carlyle admits his hero's limitations when he points our Frederick's own admissions of ambition in a letter to Voltaire. "Such are my occupations;—which I would willingly make over to another, if the Phantom they call Fame (Gloire) did not rise on me too often. In truth, it is a great folly, but a folly difficult to cast away when once you are smitten by it. 'Phantom of *Gloire* somewhat rampant in those first weeks; let us see whether it will not lay itself again, forevermore, before long'" (IV, 34). Although he is at first sensible of the flaw of ambition in his hero's character, Carlyle at length views Frederick's wars as the work he was destined to do, not as the result of his ambitions.

It was Monday 23rd, when the Siege of Neisse was abandoned, on Wednesday, Friedrich himself turns homeward; looks into Schweidnitz, looks into Liegnitz; and arrives at Berlin as the week ends,—much acclamation greeting him from the multitude. Except those Three masked Fortresses, capable of no defence to speak of, were Winter over, Silesia is all Friedrich's,—has fallen wholly to him in the space of about Seven Weeks. The seizure has been easy; but the retaining of it, perhaps he himself begins to see more clearly, will have difficulties! From this point, the talk about *gloire* nearly ceases in his Correspondence. In those seven weeks he has, with *gloire* or otherwise, cut-out for himself such a life of labour as no man of his Century had. (60)

In spite of the many evidences of his admiration for Frederick, Carlyle remains essentially judicial in his evaluation of the man. Frederick is not presented as the greatest of kings; he is only the greatest king of his century; he never reaches or even seeks the heights attained by Cromwell. Frederick is not the leader whom Carlyle offered his readers twenty years before, but he is a powerful antidote for democratic tendencies such as were sweeping Europe in 1848. With Frederick, Carlyle admits, the world does not have the best, but it has a true king who can rule with order and justice.

Carlyle points out Frederick's shortcomings with the same honesty that he praises his excellences. The greatest of Frederick's flaws was that he could not rise above his century.

"Voltaire was the spiritual complement of Freidrich," says Sauerteig once: "what little of lasting their poor Century produced lies mainly in these Two. A very somnambulating Century! But what little it *did*, we must call Friedrich; what little it *thought*, Voltaire. Other fruit we have not from it to speak of, at this day. Voltaire, and what *can* be faithfully done on the Voltaire Creed; 'Realised Voltairism';—admit it, reader, not in a too triumphant humour,—is not that pretty much the net historical product of the Eighteenth Century? The rest of its history either pure somnambulism; or a mere Controversy, to the effect, 'Realised Voltairism? How soon shall it be realised then? Not at once, surely!' So that Friedrich and Voltaire are related, not by accident only. They are, they for want of better, the two Original Men of their Century; the chief and in a sense the sole products of their Century. They alone remain to us as still living results from it,—such as they are. And the rest, truly *ought* to depart and vanish (as they are now doing); being mere ephemera; contemporary eaters, scramblers for provender, talkers of acceptable hearsay; and related merely to the butteries and wiggeries of their time, and not related to the Perennialities at all, as these Two were." (III, 177 - 78)

Frederick, then, was related to the "perennialities" even though his relationship was not the exalted one of the prophet or the poet. "Facts are a kind of divine thing to Friedrich; much more so than to common men: this is essentially what Religion I have found in Friedrich. And, let me assure you, it is an invaluable element in any man's Religion, and highly indispensable, though so often dispensed with!" (IV, 215 - 16).

The heart of Carlyle's life and times biography is the history of Frederick's wars; and these conflicts form the major subject of Volumes IV, V, VI, and VII. The descriptions of the campaigns, the pictures of the actual battles never fail to attain vividness and reality. The figure of Frederick is ever present, or if he is not in the immediate foreground, he is nearby; but these volumes, however interesting they may be as a kind of dramatic history, contribute little

to the reader's understanding of Frederick the man. They further
the understanding of Frederick's character only by demonstrating
his qualities of resourcefulness, frugality, efficiency, and swiftness.
Carlyle shows Frederick progressing from a raw general to a compe-
tent one. He demonstrates Frederick's ability to keep his country
functioning normally during the years of war. He proves to the
reader that Frederick's kingship was a true one; and if his character
does not develop into the desired magnificence of the Carlylean
hero, it must be remembered that even to Carlyle, Frederick was at
best the product of the eighteenth century.

Carlyle has completed his formula for biography long before
Frederick's growth and maturity have been depicted. At fifty-one
the great wars are over, and Frederick turns to the rebuilding of his
kingdom. Here Carlyle shows Frederick in a guise more appealing
to the present day than that of Frederick the warrior. The last
volume (VIII) is to be preferred to the four preceding which deal of
wars. Frederick is more the king when he distributes his artillery
horses among his farmers for use as plough teams. His little
successes at supplying hard-pressed subjects with food and seed
loom larger than his most successful battles, which time has proved
to have settled nothing. The contrast of rule and anarchy, monarchy
and democracy, is presented again and again for the elucidation of
his readers. "And had Friedrich no feeling about Poland itself, then,
and this atrocious Partitioning of the poor Country? Apparently
none whatever;—unless it might be, that Deliverance from
Anarchy, Pestilence, Famine, and Pigs eating your dead bodies,
would be a manifest advantage for Poland, while it was the one way
of saving Europe from war" (VIII, 115). Kingdoms existing in no-
rule or anarchy, Carlyle pointedly asserts, have a way of being par-
titioned, getting themselves proper rulers one way or another.
Other than the repetition of his lesson, Carlyle has little more to
say. He has now only to impress his readers with the fact that
Frederick had always been chiefly interested in just government.
"During all this while and to the very end, Friedrich's Affairs, great
and small, were, in every branch and item, guided on by him, with
a perfection not surpassed in his palmiest days: he saw his
Ministers, saw all who had business with him, many who had little;
and in the sore coil of bodily miseries, as Hertzberg observed with
wonder, never was the King's intellect clearer or his judgment more
just and decisive" (289).

Frederick's last years are given a mellow beauty by Carlyle's
skillful hand. Upon Frederick's death his subjects are pictured

mourning for the good king. In spite of his heavy hand, they are sad
to lose him. Even here Carlyle can not keep from adding his moral
lesson.

I define him to myself as hitherto the Last of the Kings;—when the Next
will be is a very long question: But it seems to me as if Nations, probably all
Nations, by and by, in their despair,—blinded, swallowed like Jonah, in
such a whale's belly of things brutish, waste, abominable (for is not
Anarchy, or the Rule of what is Baser over what is Nobler, the one life's
misery worth complaining of, and in fact, the abomination of abominations,
springing from the producing all others whatsoever?)—as if the Nations
universally, and England too if it hold on, may more and more bethink
themselves of such a Man and his Function and Performance, with feelings
far other than are possible at present. Meanwhile, all I had to say of him is
finished: that too, it seems was a bit of work appointed to be done. Adieu,
good readers; bad also, adieu. (300)

## V  Vignettes in Frederick

Although Frederick is the central figure of the biography, his is
not the only life pictured in this work. Excellent short lives of
Frederick's ancestors appear in the first volume. Some of them are
true gems of biography, microscopic of cut, set in such a way as best
to illuminate the trend of German history. The most complete of the
companion biographies is the life of Friedrich Wilhelm. Others that
are remembered as being effective are the sketches of Voltaire and
August the Strong. Carlyle's ability in the depiction of these
historical celebrities in minute sketches has never been surpassed.
With the deftest skill and neatest sense of fitting expression he
handles a multitude of figures, keeping each distinct from the other.
His method is that of fastening on a major characteristic or physical
trait that aptly summarizes the personality of the individual por-
trayed. There are many such portraits in Frederick the Great, but
the method used in all of them is the same. Some of them are as
simple as the following of Margaret of the Tyrol, who in 1342
married Ludwig, Kurfurst of Brandenburg:

Margaret of the Tyrol, commonly called, by contemporaries and posterity,
Maultasche (Mouthpoke, Pocket-mouth), she was the bride:—marriage
done at Innspruck, 1342, under furtherance of father Ludwig the
Kaiser:—such a mouth as we can fancy, and a character corresponding to it.
This, which seemed to the two Ludwigs a very conquest of the golden-
fleece under conditions, proved the beginning of their worst days to both of
them.

Not a lovely bride at all, this Maultasche; who is verging now towards middle life withal, and has had enough to cross her in the world. Was already married thirteen years ago; not wisely nor by any means too well. A terrible dragon of a woman. Has been in nameless domestic quarrels; in wars and sieges with rebellious vassals; claps you an iron cap on her head, and takes the field when need is: furious she-bear of the Tyrol. But she has immense possessions, if wanting in female charms. (I, 135 - 36)

Other of the life sketches done by Carlyle in this work are more detailed; some could be extracted from their settings and stand very well on their own strength.

*The History of Frederick the Great* has been sharply criticized, and it undoubtedly deserves criticism. History and biography are now fused and again only mixed. Its details are occasionally inaccurate and it is filled with moral lecturing, which, after all, was what was closest to Carlyle's purpose in writing.

### CHAPTER 10

# Reminiscences, *Letters, Last Years*

## I   Reminiscences

THE volume of writing containing Carlyle's memories of
James Carlyle, Edward Irving, Lord Jeffrey, and Jane Welsh
Carlyle, and brief notes on Southey and Wordsworth was edited
and published in 1881 by J. A. Froude under the title
*Reminiscences.* Carlyle writes of his subjects in relation to himself,
apparently with no further end in mind than to preserve for his personal satisfaction the memories of people who had seriously engaged his affections or interest.

Strictly speaking, the *Reminiscenses* lack either the purpose or
the finish that would entitle them the right to be considered among
Carlyle's literary products. On the other hand, they are evidence of
what Carlyle might have written had his purpose been different
from what it was. Whereas his motivation for writing his major
works was primarily evocative, his motivation for writing the
*Reminiscences* was expressive. All of the reminiscences express his
sense of isolation and personal loss. The essay on James Carlyle was
written following his father's death in 1832, and the pieces on Irving, Jeffrey, and Jane Welsh Carlyle were written after the death
of his wife in 1866.

Because the *Reminiscences* were occasioned by two of the
greatest losses of his life, the reader is prepared to find their tone to
be quite different from that found in works published under his
supervision; even so, one hardly expects the difference to be as
pronounced as it actually is. The apocalyptic ferver characteristic of
the works Carlyle prepared for the public is replaced by a pervading
melancholy and an encompassing sorrow that rings through his
sentences in Joblike self-reproach for his inability to give those now
dead deeper understanding and appreciation when they were alive.

The large amount of autobiographical material that they contain increases the value of these works. Carlyle appears frequently on his pages in roles rarely revealed elsewhere. In "James Carlyle," his father is seen through the eyes of the boy, the eyes of the youth, and the eyes of the man. Although Carlyle presents his father as a man who "was religious with the consent of his whole faculties" (*Reminiscences*, 16), the work does not attempt to trace his development as a hero. "He was not there to govern, but to be governed; could still live and therefore did not revolt," writes Carlyle (48). Instead, he pictures his father by means of anecdote and description as he must have lived. He recounts what he has heard of his father's youth, mentioning his poverty, his seriousness, his distrust of literature, his devotion to work and family, his caustic wit, and his lengthy silences. He tells how his father carried him as a boy, half-terrified though confident of his safety, over a narrow footbridge. He compares him to Robert Burns, judges his father the better man, and concludes: "Never, of all the men I have seen, has one come personally in my way in whom the endowment from nature and the arena from fortune were so utterly out of proportion" (15).

Though, once he began attending school at the age of ten, Carlyle was home only for visits and vacations, he responded vividly to his father's personality. He remembers that, though he disapproved of Carlyle's leaving teaching, he said, "at worst nothing never once to whisper discontent with me" (47). And he recalls that, once he became settled in his career later in life, his father "seemed prouder of me than ever." (51) But the strength of the essay rests on its anecdotes that suggest deep and powerful feelings. When his father, recovering from his first severe illness, walked out wrapped in a red plaid "to try whether he would not happen to see me coming," (48) the reader knows the presence of unspoken emotions. Or when Carlyle remembers his father's reported response to a letter and the gift of a pair of spectacles—"he was very glad and nigh weeping" (51)—the reader draws to the verge of inexpressible emotions. Such small events, growing large in Carlyle's memory, confirm his feelings of loss and desolation.

Carlyle concludes his reminiscences of his father with a characteristic statement of his own belief.

Man follows man. His life is a tale that has been told; yet under Time does there not lie Eternity? Perhaps my father, all that essentially was my father, is even now near me, with me. Both he and I were with God. Perhaps, if it so please God, we shall in some higher state of being meet one another, recognize one another. As it is written, we shall be forever with God. The possibility, nay (in some way) the certainty of perennial existence daily grows plainer to me. "The essence of whatever was, is, or shall be, even now is." God is great. God is good. His will be done, for it will be right. (51 - 52)

Scholars of religion might dispute that Carlyle's credo is authorized by Christian doctrine, but no evidence suggests that Carlyle modified the convictions he expressed in 1832, following the death of his father.

Although thirty-four years separate the reminiscences of James Carlyle from those of Edward Irving, Lord Jeffrey, and Jane Welsh Carlyle, the method and attitudes found in the later pieces are similar to those expressed in 1832. The chief distinction found in the later reminiscences is an increasing weariness with life and its cares that culminates in the self-recrimination and torment found in the pages devoted to his wife.

My noble one! I say deliberately her part in the stern battle, and except myself none knows how stern, was brighter and braver than my own. Thanks, darling, for your shining words and acts, which were continual in my eyes, and in no other mortal's. Worthless I was your divinity, wrapt in your perpetual love of me and pride in me, in defiance of all men and things. Oh, was it not beautiful, all this that I have lost forever! And I was Thomas the Doubter, the unhoping; till now the only half-believing, in myself and my priceless opulences! At my return from Annandale, after "French Revolution," she so cheerily recounted to me all the good "items;" item after item. "Oh it has had a great success, dear!"—to no purpose; and at length beautifully lost patience with me for my incredulous humour. My life has not wanted at any time what I used to call "desperate hope" to all lengths; but of common "hoping hope" it has had but little; and has been shrouded since youthhood (almost since boyhood, for my school-years, at Annan, were very miserable, harsh, barren and worse) in continual gloom and grimness, as of a man set too nakedly *versus* the devil and all men. Could I be easy to live with? She flickered round me like perpetual radiance, and in spite of my glooms and my misdoings, would at no moment cease to love me and help me. What of bounty too is in heaven! (404 - 405)

Carlyle clearly saw his life predetermined, beyond his control, if not without its blessings. He remained true to his Calvinistic beliefs to the end of his years.

The reminiscence entitled "Edward Irving" is almost equally devoted to Carlyle's own experiences, which include his associations with the Bullers, whose sons he tutored, the writing of his early works, acquaintanceship with Coleridge and Charles Lamb, sundry friendships, and his first trip to Paris. All of the *Reminiscences* reveal more of Carlyle than of his subjects. They show the Jeremiah of the nineteenth century stripped of his moral indignation. The vigorous, angry challenger of sham becomes the anguished mortal who faces the world alone when all those whom he loved are gone. They remain his most personal responses to his life. Anguished disclosures in the *Reminiscences* of Carlyle's sense of inadequacy and failure remain the best explanation for the angry and intemperate outbursts of his later years.

## II    *The Letters*

As a writer of letters, Carlyle has few superiors. During his life he wrote hundreds of letters to members of his family, to his wife, to Göethe, to Emerson, and to friends, acquaintances, and admirers. Those written to people closest to him often share the frustrations expressed in the *Reminiscences* and *Notebooks*, but most are vivid expressions of his hopes, aspirations, and concerns. When he writes to individuals, he reveals himself, to use his own words, as "an authentic human being." His deep need to communicate on a personal level, frustrated in his published writings, succeeds in his correspondence. Here, Carlyle displays unexpected depths of sympathy and concern for his fellow man.

He wrote to dwindling numbers of correspondents through 1879, and his letters are filled with comments on his reading, queries about the health of others, and statements about his own. But, as he writes to his brother in November 1878, he was growing tired: "For a long time back, I have been accustomed to look upon the *"ernsten Freund"* as the most merciful and indispensable refuge appointed by the great Creator for his wearied children whose work is done" (*New Letters*, II, 338).

## III    *Last Years*

Following the completion of the last proof sheets of *Frederick the Great* in 1865, Carlyle and his wife rested at Lady Ashburton's cottage on the seashore at Seaton. The rest, as usual, plunged him into gloom as devastating as the frustrations of writing. Summer found him in Scotland, where he rode, read, and visited old acquaintances and familiar places. His wife, who had been ill, did not accompany him.

In the fall, he reluctantly agreed to become rector of the University of Edinburgh; and in the spring of 1866, he made the trip to Edinburgh for installation to his office. His address on April 2 was a resume of his lifelong message. His topics included work, religion, history, and heroic men. He had written the same things many times over, but when he spoke them at Edinburgh, his words were acclaimed and reported with enthusiasm from one end of the country to the other.

After the ceremony at Edinburgh, he sprained his ankle and delayed his return home until it mended. His accident prevented his ever seeing his wife again, for she died April 21, while on a carriage ride. Carlyle never forgave himself for his absence at the time of her death. Characteristically, he recounted all his omissions of kindnesses during the years of their married life.

When Jane died, he was seventy-one years old. Except for "Shooting Niagara: and After," which was published in *Macmillan's Magazine* in August 1867, and *Kings of Norway,* which was mostly dictated, his writing was finished. He busied himself with corrections and revisions for the first complete edition of his works, and he wrote beautiful, compassionate letters. The employment was good for him, but it could not make him forget the painful memories of the past.

The last fifteen years of his life were not much different from all the others. He had become a famous man, and his peace was constantly interrupted by well-wishers. Froude, Allingham, and others waited upon his every desire, but he became increasingly difficult. He was lost without work. By the end of 1873, he had lost the use of his right hand. Still alert at seventy-eight, he was increasingly forced into inactivity. Great Britain offered him the Grand Cross in 1874, but he refused the honor. When he died on February 5, 1881, at the age of eighty-five, a burial place in Westminster Abbey was offered by Dean Stanley. But, as requested in his will, Carlyle was buried near his father and mother in the old kirkyard at Ecclefechan. All in all it was a better resting place, for he would not have been at peace in Westminster Abbey. He would have been disturbed by the sermons.

### CHAPTER 11

# Conclusions

CARLYLE'S biographies, histories, and essays are demonstrations of his belief in a world in which the will of God permeates all things. At no time did he write simply to entertain the reader. He consistently sees the problems of government, industry, and agriculture as extensions of moral issues. In fact, he understands art in precisely the same way, too. The poem written or the bridge built was ultimately the expression of the moral quality of the poet or builder.

## I Biographies

Carlyle's biographies fall quite naturally into two major divisions: the biographies that illustrate the individual's struggle with the forces of disorder in his life and the conquering of it or being conquered by it; and the biographies that illustrate the individual's struggles with chaos in the world of fact, spirit, or idea. Without any principle of order, a man becomes a slave to be directed by others. He is the God-forgotten and is fortunate if a more perfect personality will take charge of him and direct him toward the "everlasting verities." Personalities that proceed no further than this stage are ordinarily ignored by Carlyle; indeed, since the struggle with individual chaos is universally experienced, the resolution of chaos on this level appears in the hero's first struggle with the forces of anarchy. Because Carlyle equates order with godliness, the further the hero can proceed beyond the vanquishing of personal chaos to the creation of political, artistic, or spiritual order, the greater the man he is.

Of higher nature than the man who can attain the ordering of his own life is the man who can bring order to the lives of others. There are varying degrees of this ability, but roughly it can be divided into two minor divisions. There are men who can create order in govern-

ment, and there are men who can create order in idea. Carlyle
devoted much of his time to men who create order in government
because he believed that better government was the greatest need
of his day. His early writings, particularly the essays, are considerations of men, ordinarily poets and philosophers, who had the
highest ability of creating order in the realm of idea, where they are
directly inspired by the Infinite. As time passed, Carlyle became
more and more certain that British misgovernment would end in
national disaster. For that reason his emphasis gradually changed
from the heroes who could create order of the spirit or idea to those
who could create order in government. His early heroes were poets
and philosophers; his later heroes were governors. Cromwell
became Carlyle's ideal ruler because he fitted precisely Carlyle's
definition of the God-ordained hero. As the century wore on,
Carlyle became more certain that he would have to establish his
thesis in the face of times unfavorable to the faith of either Abbot
Samson or Cromwell. Even then it was with great hesitation that he
finally resolved to write the history of Frederick. Carlyle's com-
promise with his own conscience for the selection of Frederick as
the copestone of his work was that Frederick lived in one of the
most godless centuries known to history and that, after all,
Frederick probably did all that was possible under the circumstances.

Carlyle was sensitive to the spiritual needs of the British people,
but he was also aware that idealistic preachings to an increasingly
materialistic people were absurd. Pamphlet number eight of the
*Latter-Day Pamphlets* gives evidence of Carlyle's bitter disappointment that Great Britain could not admire anything better than what
appeared to him trifling and material. That twenty-five thousand
pounds was contributed to erect a statue to George Hudson, the
railroad magnate who was subsequently detected in fraudulent
business transactions, was a sign to Carlyle of how completely Great
Britain was devoted to the worship of Mammon.

For, in fact, there was more of real worship in the affair of Hudson than is
usual in such. The practical English mind has its own notions as to the
Supreme Excellence; knows the real from the spurious Avatar of Vishnu;
and does not worship without its reasons. The practical English mind, contemplating its divine Hudson, says with what remainder of reverence is in
it: "Yes, you are something like the Ideal of Man; you are he I would give
my right arm and leg, and accept a potbelly, with gout, and an appetite for

strong-waters, to be like! You out of nothing can make a world, or huge fortune of gold. (*LDP*, 256 - 57).

Hudson, as a nation's choice for her hero, was a far cry from Cromwell, and Carlyle angrily deprecated the times that condoned the worship of such men. It was clear to him that the chief responsibility for such materialistic taste was the world's growing republicanism.

If the world were not properly *anarchic*, this question "Who shall have a Statue?" would be one of the greatest and most solemn for it. Who is to have a Statue? means, Whom shall we consecrate and set apart as one of our sacred men? Sacred; that all men may see him, be reminded of him, and, by new example added to old perpetual precept, be taught what is real worth in man. Whom do you wish us to resemble? Him you set on a high column, that all men, looking on it, may be continually apprised of the duty you expect from them. What man to set there, and what man to refuse forevermore the leave to be set there: this, if a country were not anarchic as we say,—ruleless, given up to the rule of Chaos, in the primordial fibres of its being,—would be a great question for a country! (*LDP*, 258)

With the world in such condition, the job nearest at hand is that of reducing chaos to order. Once that is accomplished, it is much more possible that men can be directed to true worth once again. Carlyle's selection of Frederick the Great for his last hero was not a sign of decay in his idealism. It was his practical answer to what he considered a vulgar and chaotic age; it was the last treatment the doctor knew. In his last essay, "Shooting Niagara: and After?," which was published in *Macmillan's Magazine* for August 1867, Carlyle insisted, as he had always done, that democratic tendencies were the chief ills of the nation. Throughout his life, his emphasis became more and more focused upon what he considered to be the great evil of his age, democracy. The evil of anarchy must be dispelled before men can see the great beauty of the divine order.

Carlyle chose to present his life's teachings in the form of biography. Clothed in imaginative form and deepened by intuition, didacticism is one of Carlyle's most striking characteristics. Critics have long disapproved of didactic biography; since the turn of the century, they have been wary of the presence of imagination and intuition in biography as well. Pure biography, it is now thought, can be written only by a disinterested student of facts; and only pure biography has any merit. Nothing seems more sensible today; but to

Carlyle nothing seemed more absurd. Ours is the scientific ideal; Carlyle's is the literary ideal. The present-day ideal of scientific accuracy may produce biographies factually more precise, but it does not necessarily produce more readable, more convincing biographies than did Carlyle's intuitive method.

Carlyle believed in two biographical principles that damage him in twentieth century eyes. Although these principles are still accepted today, they are governed closely by the scientific method, whereas in Carlyle's works they were governed by the religious nature. Although his principles of sympathy and interpretation have caused him his greatest trouble, they are also the principles that made him a great biographer, for they actually enabled him to attain an empathy with his subject that is rare in the history of literature. Many readers have discovered that he is sometimes in factual error; and Carlyle, it is to be remembered, is expressly insistent upon the true detail throughout his long career. Scholars question the authority of one who would base judgment on faulty information. Carlyle's errors, however, are rarely damaging to the overall picture he has created, and correction of them changes his portraiture very little. As a matter of fact, Carlyle's accuracy is probably superior to that of the majority of his contemporaries.

Few biographers have not been challenged their rights to fame during the past fifty years. Harold Nicolson condemns all Victorian biographers in one fell blow.

Something like this happened to nineteenth-century biography. It all began splendidly. We had Moore and Southey and Lockhart; but then came earnestness, and with earnestness hagiography descended on us with its sullen cloud, and the Victorian biographer scribbled laboriously by the light of shaded lamps. It cannot be sufficiently emphasized that the art of biography is intellectual and not emotional. So long as the intellect is undisturbed by emotion you have good biography. The moment, however, that any emotion (such as reverence, affection, ethical desires, religious belief) intrudes upon the composition of a biography, that biography is doomed. Of all such emotions religious earnestness is the most fatal to pure biography.[1]

Lockhart, who had most of the information that he needed to write a completely accurate life of Scott, did not meet modern demands for accuracy and is condemned by H. J. C. Grierson for manipulating letters and dramatizing description of persons and events.[2] Tested by the scholarship of the present age, even the great Boswell shows faults. Joseph Wood Krutch in his *Samuel Johnson* confesses, "Just how nearly impeccable Boswell's memory was and just how closely his original notes may therefore be supposed to record Johnson's words verbatim is a question still being disputed."[3] The greatest of biographical art has been challenged by modern scholarship. "Scientific" scholarship has demonstrated that Boswell "Johnsonized" Johnson, and it worries that art is not history. Perhaps the biographers were not so remiss in accuracy as we are amiss in our determination that perfect accuracy shall have some particular virtue.

The fact remains that Carlyle has been condemned for his inaccuracy. There is no need for one to attempt a defense for Carlyle on the basis of accurate scholarship; it would be a difficult feat. On the other hand, scholarly biography gives just as slanted a picture of its subject as does the "earnest" biography of the Victorians. Only the best of both periods will stand the test of time, and it may be doubted whether that test will be either moral earnestness or detailed accuracy. Neither can give literature the perfect biography; the method that comes closest to it is probably some combination of the two. Accuracy in the matter of biographic detail seems to have little to do with the actual effectiveness of biography. It can serve as the beginning of an interpretation that may or may not be true. The truth of biographical writing depends upon the ability of the writer; it does not depend upon scholarship.

Carlyle's overevaluation of the superior man is the logical result of his particular era as well as of his background. He was born at the close of the French Revolution; his youthful years witnessed the successes of Napoleon; he was nearly twenty years old at the time of Waterloo. His decade decried the evils of the revolution just as Wordsworth's decade heralded the glories of it. The violence of the French Revolution had by 1795 blurred the Englishman's appreciation for the idealism that preceded it. As Harold Nicolson says:

We sometimes fail to realise the vast gulf which yawned between the men born before the French Revolution and those born, say, in 1795. Let me take a striking instance. A gap of not more than seven years separates the birth-year of Byron from that of Thomas Arnold. And yet, on 1st February 1819, at a moment when Arnold was wrestling with scruples about "that most awful subject—the doctrine of the blessed Trinity" ("Do not start, my dear Coleridge"), Byron at Venice was writing:

> Let not a monument give you or me hopes
> Since not a pinch of dust is left to Cheops.

Both Byron and Arnold, in their respective manners, were extreme; and yet the vast majority of Englishmen born in 1785 would have been bewildered by Arnold's earnestness, and the vast majority of Englishmen born in 1795 would have been horrified by the flippancy of Byron. For within that short decade the germ of seriousness had infected the youth of England. The malady spread with amazing rapidity; the older generation went down like ninepins.[4]

Yet Carlyle also retained something of the Romantic idea to the very end of his days. His faith in the hero is fundamentally what he could always honor of the Romantic idealization of man. The persistence of the Romantic emphasis on the worth of man can be seen in the determination with which post-Romantics retained some modified form of it. In Carlyle's case, the general disillusionment with the common man was influenced by complicating factors. As a youth Carlyle had been saturated with a strict Calvinism that taught that many were damned and few were saved. The few who were predestined to the eternal life learned of their appointment partly through their material success. Such an idea was the origin of the doctrine of hero worship. Carlyle's hero is a combination of the elect of the Calvinist and of a deterioration of the Romantic conception of the worth of man.

The abandonment of the Romantic point of view in the case of Carlyle is complicated by another factor, which in itself is basic enough to human thought but which was accentuated by the violence of the French Revolution as well as by the restlessness in Britain of the post-Napoleonic period. The fear of revolution felt by upper classes was considerable. The Peterloo Massacre, which Carlyle mentions frequently, was a direct result of it. The depopulation of the rural areas to feed the thriving mills and manufacturing centers was producing a drifting population, poverty-stricken and chaotic. The confusion perpetrated by the shift of population, the tremendous growth of the city, the unprecedented increase in population, and the depression that followed the Napoleonic wars caused serious unrest among the lower classes. Such actions naturally alarmed the more conservative property holders, who began to fear that social unrest would eventually result in serious curtailment of their property rights. Nevertheless, England met the problem by adopting democratic reforms; and Thomas Carlyle, who could see nothing but chaos resulting from democracy, spent much of his time writing to show that England had made the wrong choice. Carlyle's method of attack was to point to the various focuses of

British disorder, pronounce them evil, and declare that only the hero was able to redress them.

## II  *Histories*

Carlyle's histories share the characteristics of his biographies; they contain many biographical passages. History served Carlyle as a setting for the moral development of individual lives, and he tended to see it as the result of moral good and evil. The course of history becomes in his hands a drama between the conflicting forces of chaos and of order. Thus, he can view the French Revolution as retribution for the atheism and misgovernment of the eighteenth century. Because events and actions are metaphors of moral significance, he did not write history to let the facts speak for themselves. History proved his case for the hero and for hero worship.

Carlyle's demand for order seemed sound to many during his age and still seems reasonable to some. Certainly the violence and disorder of revolutionary periods is still terrible, but Carlyle went further than merely insisting upon orderliness. He left little doubt that he was talking of a strict form of it. Carlyle's chief failing in the eyes of the present is not that he insisted upon order as a good but that he inferred that the greatest order was the greatest good. Modern totalitarianism is uncomfortably close to Carlyle's descriptions of his beloved order; at least the twentieth century variety of it appears superficially to be as completely orderly as he could have wished. Upon experiencing it, observing it in action, we can determine that order alone is not the greatest good. Carlyle was perfectly aware of the dangers of tyranny and was careful therefore to demand renunciation from the most practical of his heroes. Carlyle was not a British Nietzsche.[5] His order is governed by the religious principles of the Calvinist. His totalitarian state would have been grim, but it would not have been depraved.

## III  *Moral Purposes*

As a biographer, Carlyle's contribution to literature was one certain to be made during the nineteenth century; if he had not made it, another must certainly have done so. Even though he saw his purpose as moral, Carlyle perfected biography as a method of propaganda. He was not by any means the first to use life-writing as propaganda, but he was certainly one of the most skilled at it. It is natural that a man like Carlyle should use biography for special pleading. His earliest literature was the Bible, in which the earliest slanted biographies are found. Although he might have obtained the idea from the Methodists, who were writing "conversion" lives in large numbers during the last half of the eighteenth century, it is more reasonable to assume that the influence for him was the scriptures. There can be little doubt that Carlyle's tendency to preach through biography was inspired by his religious background. His earnestness was partly natural to him and partly a product of his age; it is at the heart of everything that Carlyle ever wrote.

However limited the aim of Carlyle's biographies may be, they are always skillfully planned and artistically executed. He was occasionally misled by his natural sympathy or by reliance upon false facts, but he never failed to draw a believable personality. While Carlyle's delight in order often twisted his best efforts in the field of social criticism, it gave him a peculiar insight to the human personality. For in his efforts to find the ordering of a man's character, he managed to come closer to the understanding of man than any other writer of his age.

Carlyle's use of order as a key to human psychology is responsible for much of the dramatic effect he attains in his life writing. Man and chaos become adversaries in his biographies, and he points up this dramatic conflict in order to attain the greatest didactic effectiveness. But the ordinary result is not so much a greater or even a clearer teaching as it is a dramatic conflict in which the subject becomes a hero waging a battle against the relentless forces of evil that oppose him. The dramatic situation is emphasized by the high stakes. Honor and eternal salvation are his who conquers, but eternal darkness is the lot of the man who cannot resolve the chaos that confronts him. Carlyle's use of language increases the sense of conflict, and his biography becomes the story of the hero fighting forces of evil for all humanity.

If Carlyle cannot find order as an integral part of a man's life, he ordinarily avoids writing that life; occasionally, however, as in the case of Coleridge, he outlines the character briefly as a companion piece to another life. It is a rare thing indeed to find Carlyle sympathetic to a man who was unable to reduce even his own life to order. Burns was an exception.

His morality, in most of its practical points, is that of a mere worldly man; enjoyment, in a finer or coarser shape, is the only thing he longs and strives for. A noble instinct sometimes raises him above this; but an instinct only, and acting only for moments. He has no Religion; in the shallow age, where his days were cast, Religion was not discriminated from the New and Old Light *forms* of Religion; and was, with these, becoming obsolete in the minds of men. His heart, indeed, is alive with a trembling adoration, but there is no temple in his understanding. His religion, at best, is an anxious wish; like that of Rabelais, "a great Perhaps." (*Essays*, I, 313)

The danger of Carlyle's principles of sympathy and interpretation is that they are easily misapplied when they are governed by hero worship. Hero worship has produced as many poor biographies as it has good ones. Froude and Wilson were both disciples of Carlyle, yet Froude's biography is great and Wilson's is scarcely biography. Carlyle himself seems closest to hero worship when he is writing *Oliver Cromwell's Letters and Speeches*, and is farthest from hero worship when he is writing *The Life of John Sterling*. *John Sterling* remains one of the world's great biographies, and *Oliver Cromwell's Letters and Speeches* is rarely read. Hero worship, it would seem, in spite of what Carlyle wrote about Boswell, is not a requisite to good biography; on the contrary, it is often a hindrance.

## IV  *Biographical Style*

Although it took a long time to become popular, Carlyle's demand that biography be limited to the confines of one volume is today ordinarily accepted. The fact that Carlyle himself did not always follow his teaching can be explained. *Oliver Cromwell's Letters and Speeches* by its very title dictated its length. *The French Revolution* is a series of biographies, and *Frederick the Great* is biography supplemented by long passages of historical anecdotes concerning Frederick's wars. *The Life of Schiller, The Life of John Sterling, Sartor Resartus, Heroes and Hero-Worship*, and *Past and Present* are single volume works, and all are biography or are mainly biographical. It must be admitted that with respect to length, both in practice and in theory, Carlyle is closer to the twentieth century than the majority of his contemporaries.

Carlyle's influence in biography is not entirely ideal. Although his statements concerning biography are still widely approved and his own life writing, generally speaking, conforms to his biographical principles, he added thereto didacticism under the guise of interpretation. Even in his essays that deal with biography as a genre of literature, Carlyle demanded the interpretation of facts as a prerogative of the biographer. His romantic mysticism, which insisted upon looking beyond the fact for the thing in essence, might have betrayed him to extravagant interpretations had he not been an earnest man. Because he was, his tendency was to explain impenetrable facts as so willed by God. The following example is an excellent one.

There is no doubt but these are threatening times, full of risk and distress: a country agitated with political discontent, with economical embarrassment; the lower orders, straitened by want, exasperated by disappointment, all ready for *any* kind of change, whether by revolt or otherwise; nowhere any Wisdom, any Faithfulness to give them counsel; and now while the dark Winter is setting in, a pestilential malady arrived on our coasts, to carry off doubtless many into the land of Silence! Truly may we say, God's judgments are abroad on the Earth: it behoves us all, and each of us for himself to think deeply of it, and so far as strength is given us, with our whole heart, to "consider our ways and be wise." Mevertheless there is always this strong tower of Defence, that it *is* of God's ordering; that not a hair of our head, of the very meanest head, can fall to the ground without His command; and the Faith, which is the beginning and the end of Knowledge, teaches us that He commands all things *well*. (*Letters*, 264 - 65)

And so it is with personality. The poet, the priest, the prophet, in the long run, any man who distinguishes himself from the crowd becomes to Carlyle the chosen of God. His actions in some unfathomable way fulfill the command of God. Man's desire to acknowledge a god is the same desire as the desire to acknowledge order. Carlyle's deeply religious nature simply made a stronger equation of God and order than is normal. The one became for Carlyle the symbol of the will of the other.

To Carlyle the biography of a great man was modern scripture. The story of how he made order of the particular variety of chaos that confronted him is of special significance to all men because the great man and God stand in close relationship. The life of the great man, therefore, became for Carlyle the word of God upon the individual problems with which the great man was confronted. Carlyle's works, in view of his attitude toward biography, assume an added importance. Since they are primarily biographical and since biography is, in Carlyle's thinking, man's closest approach to the word of God, Carlyle's works, which are based on the lives of heroes and great men, become, in his thinking, authentic scripture.

## V *Calvinistic Radicalism*

Carlyle's seeming liberalism during his youth is little more than apparent. He thought of himself not as a liberal but as a radical; yet I believe that he intended the root meaning of the term and not its modern connotation. Carlyle never thought of trying the untried. His way was never the way of developing a new society. Carlyle's conception of his duty was that of a prophet, and his voice was that of a Jeremiah. He had not the slightest desire to lead man to something heretofore unknown. His duty was to lead man back to the ways of God; and, although much was changed in the form of religion that the word of God might assume for the nineteenth century, in essence it was for Carlyle very little different from what it had been for his own forefathers. To Charles Frederick Harrold, Carlyle's teachings all bear the stamp of his childhood religion:

All of Carlyle's social principles, we may conclude, are those of the totalitarian or corporate community, and bear the stamp of Calvin. They point to an ideal almost wholly out of time with the ground tones of the age that rejected him: The ideal of the "glorious community" where rewards are zero and the end of divine made real. It was this ideal, then, as it rose on the foundation of Calvinism, rather than any complex *a priori* theory in Fichte, Schelling, or Hegel, which haunted Carlyle and which he relentlessly presented to his contemporaries. It held up to Victorian eyes the old enchanting but eternally rejected ideal of the world as a temple, with human laws patterned after transcendent "Right," so that in the end, the world of man might become, as was the hope of that first great Calvinist, St. Augustine, a veritable City of God.[6]

Carlyle was radical in that he would turn men once again to God, or, at least, restate God's truths to man. His chief effort in life was directed to this end; but, when the age refused to listen to spiritual prophecy, Carlyle shifted his attention to the social field, which was certainly in need of godly order.

Carlyle should not be considered a very considerable innovator of German ideas, nor should he be considered as essentially a historian. He is one of the greatest literary biographers of his century. His greatness lies not in the scholarly accuracy and fullness of his work, but in the brilliance of his insight and the skill of his characterizations.

The proof as to the prominence biography had for Carlyle is everywhere visible in his writings. Without exception his works are biography or contain large portions of biographical material. Carlyle's chief motivation to write was religious and the religious motive, discoverable in the work of his earliest maturity, retains its place at the center of his work to the very end of his career. Carlyle's motivation remained unchanged, as did his literary aim and method. What has been interpreted as his abandonment of high ethical and religious standards in the acceptance of Frederick the Great as a biographical subject can now be seen to be little more than a willingness to take a lesser step in the same direction at a time at which his more abstract discourses were being disregarded. The *Latter-Day Pamphlets*, it is true, are filled with the bitter language of a man who fears that the worst is near at hand, but not, however, the language of a man disillusioned in his fondest beliefs.

Carlyle was skillful in arranging lives to fit the confines of his philosophy, and he at no time departed from his own convictions. More than any other writer in the nineteenth century he was a biographer of the spiritual growth of man. For Carlyle, man's spiritual stature was reflected in his accomplishments; therefore, Carlyle emphasized the value of success for determining what is right, often to the embarrassment of his followers. But "might makes right" is always qualified by Carlyle to read, "Might makes right with the consent of God." The might of the hero is achieved by the difficult process of *entsagen* or *selbsttödtung;* heroism is not accomplished by selfish men. If heroes become selfish at any time during their activities, they are, like Napoleon, soon punished by the hand of God. When Carlyle could not illustrate *entsagen* in the lives of heroes, he sometimes deduced the process from portraits or works and occasionally even intimated its presence without the authority of evidence.

## VI  *Summary and Conclusions*

Study of Carlyle's works has led to the conclusion that his non-biographical writings are almost as completely biographical as are the biographies. The second book of *Sartor Resartus* is almost autobiographical. Without the personality sketches contained in it, *The French Revolution* would comfortably fit between the covers of a slender volume. *Heroes and Hero-Worship* contains short soul-sketches of heroes written with the express purpose of showing the public that it was becoming remiss in its treatment of the divine hero and that the current trend in the matter of hero worship should be revised. *Past and Present* has at its heart the vivid life of Abbot Samson, the practical-minded governor of men.

Carlyle continued his battle against what he considered the forces of chaos as long as he could write. When he lost the use of his right hand late in 1873, this work stopped forever, though his mind remained active and unchanged. He yielded not a step to the trends of his time, and at the end of his long life his principal beliefs were identical with those he had held fifty years before.

He was especially irritated when he heard the ordinary cant about progress, unexampled prosperity, &c. Progress whither? he would ask, and prosperity in what? People talked as if each step which they took was in the nature of things a step upward; as if each generation was necessarily wiser and better than the one before; as if there was no such thing as progressing down to hell; as if human history was anything else but a history of birth and death, advance and decline, of rise and fall, in all that men have ever made or done. The only progress to which Carlyle would allow the name was moral progress; the only prosperity the growth of better and nobler men and women: and as humanity could only expand into high dimensions in an organic society when the wise ruled and the ignorant obeyed, the progress which consisted in destroying authority, and leaving everyone to follow his own will and pleasure, was progress down to the devil and his angels. That, in his opinion, was the evident goal of the course in which we were all hurrying on such high spirits. Of the theory of equality of voting, the good and the bad on the same level, Judas Iscariot and Paul of Tarsus counting equal at the polling booth, the annals of human infatuation, he used to say, did not contain the equal.[7]

As he persisted in his distrust of democracy, he continued in his Calvinistic belief in the necessity of God's approval before success in any venture could be achieved. Froude reports the following as Carlyle's final statement on the matter:

With respect to that poor heresy of might being the symbol of right "to a certain great and venerable author," I shall have to tell Lecky one day that quite the converse or *reverse* is the great and venerable author's real opinion—namely, that right is the eternal symbol of might: as I hope he, one day descending miles and leagues beyond his present philosophy, will, with amazement and real gratification, discover; and that, in fact, he probably never met with a son of Adam more contemptuous of might except where it rests on the above origin.[8]

Some problems concerning Carlyle remain unsolved. Studies of his personal relations, including those with Edward Irving; Lord

Jeffrey, editor of the *Edinburgh Review;* Göethe; Emerson; Lady Asburton; his wife, Jane Welsh; and his parents might throw some light on his complex personality. The significance of his work, however, will not be altered greatly by such studies. Thomas Carlyle will be remembered as the last great literary figure who, following the example set by Milton, attempted to demonstrate to an increasingly materialistic society the working of divine will in human life and human society.

# Notes and References

## Chapter One

1. William Wordsworth, "Michael," in *English Romantic Poetry and Prose*, Ed. Russell Noyes (New York, 1956), 11. 443 - 47.
2. W. E. Lunt, *History of England* (New York, 1956), p. 568. Acts of parliament called "enclosure acts" required owners to fence their property.
3. Oliver Goldsmith, "The Deserted Village," in *English Romantic Poetry and Prose*, 11. 303 - 308.
4. John Keats, "To One Who Has Been Long in City Pent," in *English Romantic Poetry and Prose*.
5. William Shakespeare, "The Merchant of Venice," in *Shakespeare: The Complete Works*, Ed. G. B. Harrison (New York, 1968), III, i, 56 - 66.
6. Michael Montaigne, "Apologie of Raymond Sebond," in *The Essays of Michael, Lord of Montaigne*, trans. John Florio, 3 vols. (London, 1910), II, 170.
7. Robert Burns, "Is There for Honest Poverty," in *English Romantic Poetry and Prose*, 11. 38 - 40.
8. John Locke, "An Essay Concerning Human Understanding," in *Masterworks of Philosophy*, Ed. S. E. Frost, Jr. (New York, 1946), p. 367.

## Chapter Two

1. *Reminiscenses*, Ed. James Anthony Froude (New York, 1881), p. 17. Further references are given in the text.
2. James Anthony Froude, *Thomas Carlyle, A History of the First Forty Years of His Life: 1795 - 1835*, 2 vols. (London, 1882), I, 18. Referred to hereafter as Froude, *Life*.
3. *Sartor Resartus: The Life and Opinions of Herr Teufelsdröckh*, vol. I in *The Works of Thomas Carlyle*, Ed. H. D. Traill, 30 vols. (New York, 1896 - 1901), p. 90. All references to Carlyle's works, unless otherwise specified, are to this edition. Further references will be given in the text.
4. *Early Letters of Thomas Carlyle*, ed. Charles Eliot Norton (London, 1886), p. 10. Further references will be given in the text.
5. Froude, *Life*, I, 46.
6. David Alec Wilson, *Carlyle Till Marriage* (1795 - 1826) (London, 1923), p. 195.
7. *Two Notebooks of Thomas Carlyle, from 23d March 1822 to 16th May 1832*, Ed. Charles Eliot Norton (New York, 1898), pp. 55 - 56. Further references will be given in the text.

8. *The Love Letters of Thomas Carlyle and Jane Welsh*, Ed. Alexander Carlyle, 2 vols. (London, 1909), II, 380.

9. Froude, I, 329 - 30.

### Chapter Three

1. *Critical and Miscellaneous Essays*, 5 vols., vols. XXVI - XXX in *The Works of Thomas Carlyle*, Ed. H. D. Traill, 30 vols. (New York, 1896 - 1901), I, 210.

2. For interpretations of Carlyle's thought as Naziism, see H. J. C. Grierson, *Carlyle and Hitler* (Cambridge, 1933); and Eric Russell Bentley, *A Century of Hero-Worship* (Philadelphia, 1944).

3. *Latter-Day Pamphelts*, vol. XX in *The Works of Thomas Carlyle*, Ed. H. D. Traill, 30 vols. (New York, 1896 - 1901). These essays will be referred to hereafter as *LDP*. Further references are given in the text.

### Chapter Four

1. For a view that evaluates Carlyle's work as history, see Louise Merwin Young, *Thomas Carlyle and the Art of History* (Philadelphia, 1939).

### Chapter Five

1. Traill, Introduction, *Sartor Resartus*, vol. I in *Works*, p. xviii.

2. Moncure Daniel Conway, *Thomas Carlyle* (New York, 1881), pp. 42 - 45.

3. Froude, I, 101.

4. *Sartor Resartus*, ed. Charles Frederick Harrold (New York, 1937), pp. xxxi - ii.

### Chapter Six

1. *The Correspondence of Thomas Carlyle and Ralph Waldo Emerson*, 1834 - 1872, Ed. Charles Eliot Norton, 2 vols. (Boston, 1883), I, 12. Hereafter cited as *Correspondence*, Emerson. Further references are given in the text.

2. A. H. Everett, "Thomas Carlyle, *Sartor Resartus* in Three Books," *The North American Review*, XLI (1835), 459.

3. For detailed analysis of the influence of German writers on Carlyle, see Charles Frederick Harrold, *Carlyle and German Thought: 1819 - 1834*, *Yale Studies in English*, LXXXII (New Haven, 1934).

4. *Letters of Thomas Carlyle to John Stuart Mill, John Sterling and Robert Browning*, Ed. Alexander Carlyle (London, 1923), pp. 191 - 192.

5. James Anthony Froude, *Thomas Carlyle, A History of His Life in London, 1834 - 1881*, 2 vols, in 1 (New York, 1884), I, 35.

6. *Letters of Thomas Carlyle, 1826 - 1836*, Ed. Charles Eliot Norton (London, 1889), p. 174.

7. Henry David Thoreau, "Thomas Carlyle and His Works," *The Writings of Henry David Thoreau*, Riverside Edition, 10 vols. (Boston, 1894 - 1895), X, 100.

8. Froude, *Life*, II, 248.

9. *Ibid.*, I, 397.

10. See *Sartor Resartus*, Ed. Archibald MacMechin (Boston, 1897), pp. xlii - lx, who points out many similarities between the style of Carlyle and that of other writers.

11. *The Life of John Sterling*, vol. XI in *The Works of Thomas Carlyle*, Ed. H. D. Traill, 30 vols. (New York, 1896 - 1901), p. 155. Further references will be given in the text.

12. *Heroes and Hero-Worship*, vol. V in *The Works of Thomas Carlyle*, Ed. H. D. Traill, 30 vols. (New York, 1896 - 1901), p. 43, hereafter cited as HW. Further references will be given in the text.

### Chapter Seven

1. *The Life of Schiller*, vol XXV in *The Works of Thomas Carlyle*, Ed. H. D. Traill, 30 vols. (1896 - 1901). Further references will be given in the text, cited hereafter as *Schiller*.

2. *Correspondence between Göethe and Carlyle*, Ed. Charles Eliot Norton (London, 1887), p. 22.

3. Oliver Cromwell's Letters and Speeches, 4 vols., vols. VI - IX in *The Works of Thomas Carlyle*, Ed. H. D. Traill, 30 vols. (1896 - 1901). Further references will be given in the text, cited hereafter as *OC*.

4. Today, many readers accept the worst possible implications of Carlyle's language without question. See, for example, *Thomas Carlyle, The Nigger Question; John Stuart Mill, The Negro Question*, Ed. Eugene R. August (New York, 1971), p. xiv.

### Chapter Eight

1. *The French Revolution: A History*, 3 vols. Vols. II - IV in *The Works of Thomas Carlyle*, Ed. H. D. Traill, 30 vols. (1896 - 1901), I, 48. Further references will be given in the text, cited as *FR*.

2. *Past and Present*, vol. X in *The Works of Thomas Carlyle*, Ed. H. D. Traill, 30 vols. (1896 - 1901), p. 3. Further references will be given in the text, cited as *PP*.

### Chapter Nine

1. David Alex Wilson, *Carlyle at His Zenith* (London, 1927), p. 388.

2. James Anthony Froude places the date of this manuscript in 1852. See Froude, *Life*, II, 8.

3. *Ibid.*, pp. 10 - 11.

4. *Ibid.*, pp. 12 - 13.

5. *Ibid.*, pp. 15 - 17.

6. Conway, p. 121.

7. *Ibid.*, pp. 105 - 106.

8. Norwood Young, *Carlyle: His Rise and Fall* (London, 1927), p. 294.

9. *New Letters of Thomas Carlyle*, Ed. Alexander Carlyle, 2 vols. (London & New York, 1904), II, 142. Further references will be given in the text.

10. From a letter to Thomas Erskine, dated March 24, 1848. See Froude, *Life in London*, I, 367.

11. First trip, August 28, 1852, to September 13, 1852; second trip, August 21, 1858, to September 22, 1858.

12. *History of Frederick II of Prussia, called Frederick The Great*, 8 vols., vols. XII - XIX in *The Works of Thomas Carlyle*, Ed. H. D. Traill, 30 vols (New York, 1896 - 1901), I, 2.

13. Carlyle is at variance with Reddaway, who writes, "His first education made him a rebel; his second a hypocrite. Katte's death had taught him once and for all that life would be tolerable only if he gained his father's confidence. To this end he applied every art which a fertile brain could devise and an unscrupulous actor could practise." William Fiddian Reddaway, *Frederick the Great and the Rise of Prussia* (New York, 1908), p. 40.

### Chapter Eleven

1. Harold Nicolson, *The Development of English Biography* (New York, 1928), pp. 110 - 11.

2. H. J. C. Grierson, *Lang, Lockhart and Biography* (London, 1934), pp. 25 - 26.

3. Joseph Wood Krutch, *Samuel Johnson* (New York, 1944), p. 388.

4. Nicolson, pp. 112 - 13.

5. For a comparison of Carlyle and Nietzsche, see Bentley, pp. 153 - 62.

6. Charles Frederick Harrold, "The Nature of Carlyle's Calvinism," Studies in Philology, XXXII (July 1936), 475 - 86.

7. Froude, *Life in London*, II, 388.

8. *Ibid.*, p. 360.

# Selected Bibliography

Unless specified, all references to the works of Carlyle are to *The Works of Thomas Carlyle*. Centenary Edition. Edited with introductions by Henry Duff Traill. 30 vols. New York: Charles Scribner's Sons, 1896 - 1901.

Vol. 1. *Sartor Resartus: The Life and Opinions of Herr Teufelsdröckh.* (orig. pub. 1831)
Vols. 2 - 4. *The French Revolution: A History.* (orig. pub. 1837)
Vol. 5. *Heroes and Hero-Worship.* (orig. pub. 1841)
Vols. 6 - 9. *Oliver Cromwell's Letters and Speeches, with elucidations.* (orig. pub. 1845)
Vol. 10. *Past and Present.* (orig. pub. 1843)
Vol. 11. *The Life of John Sterling.* (orig. pub. 1851)
Vols. 12 - 19. *History of Frederick II of Prussia, called Frederick the Great.* (orig. pub. 1858 - 1865)
Vol. 20. *Latter-Day Pamphlets* (orig. pub. 1850)
Vols. 21 - 22. *German Romance: Translations from the German with Biographical and Critical Notices.* (orig. pub. 1827)
Vols. 23 - 24. *Wilhelm Meister's Apprenticeship and Travels, Translated from the German of Goethe.* (orig. pub. 1824)
Vol. 25. *The Life of Friedrich Schiller, Comprehending an Examination of His Works.* (orig. pub. 1825)
Vols. 26 - 30. *Critical and Miscellaneous Essays.*

Letters, journals, notebooks, fragments, reminiscences, and other editions are listed by date of publication.

*Reminiscences.* Edited by James Anthony Froude. New York: Charles Scribner's Sons, 1881.
*Reminiscences of My Irish Journey in 1849.* Preface, James Anthony Froude. London: Sampson, Low, Marston, Searle & Rivington, 1882.
*The Correspondence of Thomas Carlyle and Ralph Waldo Emerson, 1834 - 1872,* Edited by Charles Eliot Norton. 2 vols. Boston: James R. Osgood, 1883.
*Letters and Memorials of Jane Welsh Carlyle.* Edited by James Anthony Froude. 2 vols. New York: Charles Scribner's Sons, 1883.
*Early Letters of Thomas Carlyle, 1814 - 1826.* Edited by Charles Eliot Norton. London: Macmillan, 1886.

*Correspondence between Goethe and Carlyle*. Edited by Charles Eliot Norton. London: Macmillan, 1887.

*Letters of Thomas Carlyle, 1826 - 1836*. Edited by Charles Eliot Norton. London: Macmillan, 1889.

*Last Words of Thomas Carlyle*. London: Longmans, Green, 1892.

*Sartor Resartus*. Edited by Archibald MacMechan. Boston: Ginn, 1897.

*Two Notebooks of Thomas Carlyle, from 23d March 1822 to 16th May 1832*. Edited by Charles Eliot Norton. New York: The Grolier Club, 1898.

*Letters of Thomas Carlyle to his Youngest Sister*. Edited by Charles Townsend Copeland. Boston: Houghton, Mifflin, 1899.

*Historical Sketches of Notable Persons and Events in the Reigns of James I and Charles I*. Edited by Alexander Carlyle. London: Chapman and Hall, 1902.

*Collectanea, Thomas Carlyle*. Edited by Samuel Arthur Jones. Canton, Penn.: The Kirgate Press, 1903.

*New Letters of Thomas Carlyle*. Edited by Alexander Carlyle. 2 vols. New York: John Lane, 1904.

*The Love Letters of Thomas Carlyle and Jane Welsh*. Edited by Alexander Carlyle. 2 vols. London: John Lane, 1908.

*Letters of Thomas Carlyle to John Stuart Mill, John Sterling and Robert Browning*. Edited by Alexander Carlyle. New York: Frederick A. Stokes, 1923.

*Sartor Resartus*. Edited by Charles Frederick Harrold. New York: The Odyssey Press, 1937.

*Journey to Germany, Autumn, 1858*. Edited by Richard Albert Edward Brooks. New Haven: Yale University Press, 1940

*Letters of Thomas Carlyle to William Graham*. Edited by John Graham, Jr. Princeton, N.J.: Princeton University Press, 1950.

*Thomas Carlyle, The Nigger Question; John Stuart Mill, The Negro Question*. Edited by Eugene R. August. New York: Appleton, Century, Crofts, 1971.

SECONDARY SOURCES

ALLINGHAM, WILLIAM. *A Diary*. Edited by H. Allingham and D. Radford. London: Macmillan, 1907. Anecdote as told by a companion of Carlyle's old age.

BAKER, JOSEPH ELLIS. "Carlyle Rules the Reich." *The Saturday Review of Literature*, X (November 25, 1933), 291. An item partly responsible for Carlyle's reputation as a Nazi.

BENTLEY, ERIC RUSSELL. *A Century of Hero-Worship*. Philadelphia: J. B. Lippencott, 1944. An attack on hero worship as exemplified by Carlyle, Nietzsche, Wagner, Shaw, and others.

BROOKS, GARY H. *The Rhetorical Form of Carlyle's Sartor Resartus*

Berkeley: University of California Press, 1972. This study presents the evidence for regarding the style of *Sartor Resartus* as a synthesis of its topic and subjective elements in Carlyle's life.

CALDER, GRACE J. *The Writing of Past and Present: A Study of Carlyle's Manuscripts.* Yale Studies in English. Vol. 112. New Haven: Yale University Press, 1949. A study of Carlyle's method of composition.

COLLIS, JOHN STEWART. *The Carlyles: A Biography of Thomas and Jane Carlyle.* New York: Dodd, Mead, 1971. A biography that places emphasis on the Carlyle marriage.

CONWAY, MONCURE DANIEL. *Thomas Carlyle.* New York: Harper, 1881. A life written by an acquaintance of Carlyle after 1863.

CARLYLE, ALEXANDER and SIR JAMES CRICHTON-BROWNE. *The Nemesis of Froude.* New York: John Lane, The Bodley Head, 1903. Attack on J. A. Froude, Carlyle's biographer.

DUFFY, SIR CHARLES GAVAN. *Conversations with Carlyle.* New York: Charles Scribner's Sons, 1892. Anecdotes and letters by an Irish correspondent.

DUNN, WALDO HILARY. *Froude and Carlyle.* London: Longmans, Green, 1933. A study of the Froude controversy.

DYER, ISAAC WATSON. *A Bibliography of Thomas Carlyle's Writings and Ana.* Portland, Me.: The Southworth Press, 1928. Fine on material before 1928.

EVERETT, A. H. "Thomas Carlyle, *Sartor Resartus*, in Three Books." *The North American Review*, XLI (1835) 454 - 82. An early critical response to *Sartor Resartus.*

FROUDE, JAMES ANTHONY. *Thomas Carlyle, A History of the First Forty Years of his Life, 1795 - 1835.* 2 vols. London: Longmans, Green, 1882. Detailed and controversial life of Carlyle.

———. *Thomas Carlyle, A History of his Life in London, 1834 - 1881.* 2 vols. in 1. New York: Charles Scribner's Sons, 1884. Later life of Carlyle.

———. *My Relations with Carlyle.* London: Longmans, Green, and Co., 1903. Notes by Froude, published by Ashley A. Froude and Margaret Froude, added to the controversy over the life by Froude.

GRIERSON, H. J. C. *Carlyle and Hitler.* Cambridge, Cambridge University Press, 1933. Grierson relates Carlyle's thought to that of Nazi Germany.

———. *Lang, Lockhart and Biography.* London: Oxford University Press, 1934. A study of biographical methods.

HANSON, LAWRENCE and ELIZABETH. *Necessary Evil: The Life of Jane Welsh Carlyle.* New York: Macmillan, 1952. A detailed biography of Carlyle's wife.

KRUTCH, JOSEPH WOOD. *Samuel Johnson.* New York: Henry Holt, 1944. Contains useful commentary on biographical method.

LA VALLEY, ALBERT J. *Carlyle and the Idea of the Modern: Studies in*

*Carlyle's Prophetic Literature and its Relation to Blake, Nietzsche, Marx and Others.* New Haven: Yale University Press, 1968. A study that relates Carlyle to the present through his explorations of self.

LEA, FRANK A. *Carlyle: Prophet of Today.* London: George Routledge, 1943. Defends Carlyle's interest in reform of faith.

LEHMAN, B. H. *Carlyle's Theory of the Hero: Its Source, Development, History, and Influence on Carlyle's Work.* Durham, N. C.: Duke University Press, 1928. A tracing and analysis of Carlyle's theory of the hero.

LEVINE, GEORGE LEWIS. *The Boundaries of Fiction: Carlyle, Macaulay, Newman.* Princeton, N.J.: Princeton University Press, 1968. A study of artistic and fictional techniques in works of expository nature.

LUNT, W. E. *History of England.* New York: Harper and Row, 1956. A useful social history.

*Masterworks of Philosophy.* Ed. S. E. Frost, Jr. Garden City, N. Y.: Doubleday, 1946.

MONTAIGNE, MICHAEL. *The Essays of Michael, Lord of Montaigne,* tr. John Florio. 3 vols. London: J. M. Dent, 1910.

NEFF, EMERY. *Carlyle.* New York: W. W. Norton, 1932. A scholarly treatment of the life and works of Carlyle.

———. *Carlyle and Mill: An Introduction to Victorian Thought.* 2nd ed. rev. New York: Columbia University Press, 1926. A study of two radically different thinkers.

NICHOL, JOHN. *Carlyle.* English Men of Letters. New York: Harper, 1901.

NICOLSON, HAROLD. *The Development of English Biography.* New York: Harcourt Brace, 1928. A treatment of biographical theory and practice.

RALLI, AUGUSTUS. *Guide to Carlyle.* 2 vols. London: George Allen & Unwin, 1920. Summaries of Carlyle's works.

REDDAWAY, WILLIAM FIDDIAN. *Frederick the Great and the Rise of Prussia.* New York: G. P. Putnam, 1908.

SHINE, HILL. *Carlyle and the Saint Simonians.* Baltimore: The Johns Hopkins Press, 1941. Carlyle's relations with a French sociopolitical movement.

STAUFFER, DONALD A. *The Art of Biography in Eighteenth Century England.* 2 vols. Princeton, N.J.: Princeton University Press, 1941. A study of the development of biography and biographical theory.

SYMONS, JULIAN. *Thomas Carlyle: The Life and Ideas of a Prophet.* New York: Oxford University Press, 1952. A life that places emphasis on Carlyle's personality.

TENNYSON, G. B. *Sartor Called Resartus: The Genesis, Structure, and Style of Thomas Carlyle's First Major Work.* Princeton, N.J.: Princeton University Press, 1965. An essential document in the study of Carlyle's style.

*Thomas Carlyle: The Critical Heritage.* ed. Jules Paul Seigel. New York: Barnes & Noble, 1971. A collection of responses to Thomas Carlyle and his works by his contemporaries.

WELLEK, RENE. "Carlyle and the Philosophy of History." *The Philological Quarterly*, XXIII (January 1944), 55 - 76.

WILSON, DAVID ALEC. *Carlyle*. 6 vols. London: Kegan Paul, Trench, Trubner, 1923 - 1934.

Vol 1. *Carlyle Till Marriage* (1795 - 1826). 1923.

Vol 2. *Carlyle To "The French Revolution"* (1826 - 1837). 1924.

Vol 3. *Carlyle on Cromwell and Others* (1837 - 1848). 1925.

Vol 4. *Carlyle at His Zenith* (1848 - 1853). 1927.

Vol 5. *Carlyle to Threescore-and-Ten* (1853 - 1865). 1929.

Vol 6. *Carlyle in Old Age* (1865 - 1881). 1934. (Completed in 1934 by David Wilson MacArthur after the death of D. A. Wilson in 1933.)

A detailed life, including much anecdote.

————. *Mr. Froude and Carlyle. London: William Heinemann, 1898.* Wilson's view of the Carlyle-Froude controversy.

YOUNG, LOUISE MERWIN. *Thomas Carlyle and the Art of History.* Philadelphia: University of Pennsylvania Press, 1939. A study that treats Carlyle's works as history.

YOUNG, NORWOOD. *Carlyle: His Rise and Fall.* London: Duckworth, 1927. A treatment of negative elements in Carlyle's works.

# Index

(The works of Carlyle are listed under his name)

**DATE DUE**

| | | | |
|---|---|---|---|
| | | | |
| | | | |
| | | | |
| | | | |
| | | | |
| | | | |
| | | | |
| | | | |
| | | | |
| | | | |
| | | | |
| | | | |
| | | | |
| | | | |
| | | | |
| | | | |